THE 24 HOUR BUSINESS

THE 24 HOUR BUSINESS

Maximizing Productivity Through Round-the-Clock Operations

Richard M. Coleman

amacom

American Management Association

New York • Atlanta • Boston • Chicago • Kansas City • San Francisco • Washington, D. C.
Brussels • Mexico City • Tokyo • Toronto

This book is available at a special
discount when ordered in bulk quantities.
For information, contact Special Sales Department,
AMACOM, a division of American Management Association,
1601 Broadway, New York, NY 10019.

This publication is designed to provide accurate and authoritative
information in regard to the subject matter covered. It is sold with
the understanding that the publisher is not engaged in rendering
legal, accounting, or other professional service. If legal advice or other
expert assistance is required, the services of a competent professional
person should be sought.

Library of Congress Cataloging-in-Publication Data

Coleman, Richard M. (Richard Mark)
     The 24-hour business: maximizing productivity through round-the-
clock operations / Richard M. Coleman.
         p.   cm.
     Includes bibliographical references and index
     ISBN 0-8144-0240-2
     1. Industrial productivity.   2. Shift systems.   3. Industrial
efficiency.   4. Scheduling (Management)   5. Production control.
I. Title.
HD56.C65   1995
658.5'15—dc20   95-5703
                                                                              CIP

Printing number

10   9   8   7   6

Contents

Preface

I decided to write this book to help companies deal with a new reality in the workplace—that of the 24-hour business. If you are already a 24-hour business, this book will show you a better way to reduce costs and improve the morale, health, and safety of your employees. If you are not, this book will help you determine whether you should be so that you can reap the benefits of utilizing time to its fullest, a resource that's much cheaper than adding new equipment or people.

I realize I have an unusual occupation as a shift work consultant. How did I come to it? Although I worked the occasional shift job as a glass packer, dishwasher, postal worker, and truck unloader and spent several years as an all-night sleep technician, I didn't give shift work much thought until 1979, when I was director of the Sleep Disorder Clinic at Stanford University Medical School in California. There, I saw many shift workers who came to our clinic with numerous health problems. After doing complete physiological monitoring of them, I found that they were just as normal as you and me except for one thing—their work schedule. When I asked them what schedules they worked, I realized their problems were caused by the schedule itself. That's when the lightbulb went on. Furthermore, I discovered that the shift workers accepted working 14 out of 15 days, 16-hour shifts, and odd rotations as just a normal part of life.

In the early 1980s I had the opportunity to do research studies at a few shift work facilities to improve schedules. The initial emphasis was on health and safety, but I found out early on that better schedules could also help employee morale and improve business profitability. That's when I "hung up a shingle," and after hiring a group of enthusiastic engineers with outgoing personalities, started a shift work consulting business. During the past 15 years my colleagues and I have talked to more shift workers, shift work managers, and union leaders about 24-hour scheduling than anyone else in the world. In *The 24-Hour Business*, I share information that will improve shift work for everyone involved—managers, shift workers and their families, and even the shareholders who invest in 24-hour businesses.

Acknowledgments

Thanks to all of the employees of Coleman Consulting Group in the United States and in Australia for sharing their experiences with me. I also thank the shift workers, managers, and union officials with whom we have worked throughout the world. I am especially grateful to Kathy Amrhein, Jim Cox, Alex Heady, Karl Meyers, Tom Meyers, Carolyn Peterson, Mac Robertson, Richard Scallan, and Clyde Williams. Special thanks go to Deana Bolton for her tenaciousness in keeping this project on track, Dennis Murphy for his contribution to and review of the manuscript, and Deanna Walsh for her insights and judgment.

My sincere appreciation to the editorial team at AMACOM, who worked with me on this book: Adrienne Hickey, Jacqueline Laks Gorman, Mike Sivilli, Beverly Miller, Erica Buneo, and Judy Lopatin.

THE 24 HOUR BUSINESS

1
Good Schedules Save Millions of Dollars

The benefits of 24-hour operations are not restricted to periods of high product demand or never-put-out-the-fire industries (steel mills, refineries, power plants). The demand for 24-hour operations is widespread and growing in many hospitals, communications, transportation, supermarket, retail, insurance, computer operations, and other service industries. Companies faced with deciding how to expand to international markets, open new plants or close old ones, increase productivity without purchasing new capital equipment, and meeting customer requests just in time are considering 24-hour operations. As information access expands and a global economy becomes a reality, more and more businesses will move to shift work.

Shift workers and shift work managers are practical people; they want the answer—the ideal schedule—and they want it now! Well, here it is. If you are a shift work manager, you should run your business 24 hours a day, 365 days a year, without overtime or idle time and with your best equipment on line except while performing preventive maintenance. Your ideal schedule would look like this:

M	T	W	T	F	S	S
24	24	24	24	24	24	24

If you are a shift worker, the answer is to stay home but get a full pay check, including overtime. Your ideal schedule would look like this:

M	T	W	T	F	S	S
-	-	-	-	-	-$$	-$$

But satisfying business needs and employee desires is not enough. You also need to fulfill health and safety requirements. To maximize health and safety, shifts should be short in duration, separated by days off to recuperate, and occur during the peak period of our biological day. A schedule that looks like this:

M	T	W	T	F	S	S
10:00 A.M.– Noon	10:00 A.M.– Noon	-	10:00 A.M.– Noon	10:00 A.M.– Noon	-	-

But in the real world, the answer is more complex. The schedule that turned out to be the answer for one of our clients is shown in Figure 1-1. As you can see, the schedule is very complicated. It requires twelve regular crews plus two supplemental crews (one for service and one for maintenance). Some of the crews work days, others work nights, and the shift lengths are either 8 hours or 10 hours. Days off also vary. In our scheduling terminology (described fully in Chapter 5), we call this schedule a 110-38.3, unbalanced, 12 crews plus 2 supplemental crews, 10 and 8, rotating, super long break. Arriving at such a schedule is not easy, but this book will help you understand the process of determining what your schedule should be and how to implement it.

If you successfully blend business needs, employee desires, and health and safety requirements, you will find the right schedule. Figure 1-2 illustrates how these three elements, when engineered with scheduling technology,* can provide what we call the

---

*Coleman Consulting Group, Inc.'s technology includes a database of models (a system for deploying capital and personnel with a key operations concept), and schedules (set pattern with employee buy-in and work, pay, and coverage policies

Figure 1-1. The best cost schedule for one client.

Crew/ Week	M	T	W	T	F	S	S
1	N	N	–	N	N	–	–
2	–	–	–	D	D	D	–
3	–	D	D	D	D	–	–
4	D	D	D	–	–	–	–
5	N	N	N	N	N	–	–
6	N	N	N	–	–	–	–
7	D	D	D	D	D	–	–
8	–	–	–	D	D	D	–
9	–	–	N	N	N	–	–
10	N	N	N	N	N	–	–
11	D	D	D	–	–	–	–
12	D	D	D	D	D	–	
Service	n8	n8	n8	n8	n8	–	–
Maintenance	a8	a8	a8	a8	a8	–	

N = 4:00 P.M.–2:00 A.M.
D = 7:00 A.M.–5:00 P.M.
n8 = 12:30 A.M.–8:30 A.M.
a8 = 4:00 P.M.–midnight

Best Cost Schedule. (These three circles will be referred to repeatedly throughout this book.) Because of the importance of these elements, Chapters 2, 3, and 4 are devoted exclusively to each one, so you can determine the building blocks for your own best cost schedule. Chapter 5 teaches you how to understand schedules

tailored to that schedule), along with business, employee, and health and safety statistics for each. In addition, we've done over 150,000 shift-worker interviews totalling more than 4 million data points.

Figure 1-2. The key schedule design elements for a best cost schedule.

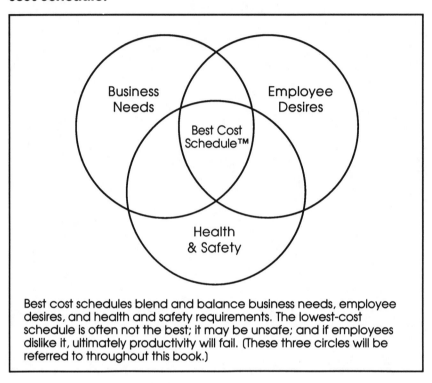

Best cost schedules blend and balance business needs, employee desires, and health and safety requirements. The lowest-cost schedule is often not the best; it may be unsafe; and if employees dislike it, ultimately productivity will fail. (These three circles will be referred to throughout this book.)

such as Figure 1-1, and Chapter 6 shows you how to implement them.

The Best Cost Schedule Versus the Wrong Schedule

In contrast to this engineered approach to achieving the Best Cost Schedule, most schedules are copied from another operation, based on tradition, or the result of a contract negotiation that probably took place far from your site. Schedules often simply grow more or less on their own, with only the most cursory planning. If you are like most other managers, you probably don't give much thought to your schedule until a crisis develops—and then you're likely to implement the first solution that comes along as quickly as possible (often based on an employee petition). These approaches are unlikely to identify the Best Cost Schedule for your business and, worse, may result in costly mistakes.

The Wall Street Journal recently reported that poorly designed schedules in 24-hour businesses cost the United States $75 billion a year in lower productivity and accidents. Lots of small mistakes add up to big numbers. For example, at a small manufacturing plant in Ohio with 250 employees, we identified $4.2 million in yearly cost savings plus a onetime capital deferment savings of $15 million by implementing the Best Cost Schedule:

Improvement	Annual Savings
Increase in utilization of most efficient equipment	$ 2,500,000
Increase in direct work units per hour	700,000
Increased part quality	400,000
Reduction in overtime	200,000
Reduced idle time	400,000
Total	$ 4,200,000
Deferred capital expenditures	15,000,000

Many 24-hour businesses accept their schedule. If there is no crisis, there is no consideration given to changing the schedule. Because of inertia and lack of awareness of alternatives, the principle of continuous improvement is rarely applied to work scheduling. We have found that most businesses that stick with traditional schedules are really accepting built-in hidden costs, such as these:

- Reduced productivity
- Low capital utilization (too much downtime)
- Excess capital purchases
- High overtime and idle time
- Poor integration of maintenance/operations
- Inefficient relief systems

- Poor communication between and integration of day workers/shift workers
- Skill imbalance
- Low training efficiency
- Lack of a shift work team concept
- Difficulty matching changing workload
- Low employee morale
- Constant bidding out of shift work
- Reduced alertness, health, and safety
- Management/labor strife
- Excessive start-ups and shutdowns

Convert these items into dollar savings. Some costs are hard, some are soft. If the total is significant for your business, consider improving your work schedule now instead of waiting for a crisis, when you will have less flexibility and time to consider your best choices. We've seen companies succeed and fail at implementation. In Chapter 6 we will review strategies for successfully implementing schedule changes and describe the steps to take, especially in difficult situations.

Although most managers are experts on their own schedule system, they usually have little training or knowledge about alternative scheduling. A common misconception is that for a given industry, one schedule will fit all solutions. But this is not the case. For example, a large energy corporation in western Australia won an industrial dispute allowing it to implement 7-day-a-week, 12-hour shifts in its eleven locations. Corporate management insisted that all eleven sites implement this schedule. Predictably, the schedule is working out in two locations, but in several others productivity has plummeted and costs have soared.

Another common misconception is that all schedules are pretty much the same. A hastily designed (wrong) 10-hour shift at Homestake Mining Co., Inc., decreased productivity; the best cost 10-hour shift improved productivity 16 percent. A BHP Minerals International mine improved productivity 14.3 percent by going from its traditional 8-hour schedule to a modified 8-hour schedule system within its union contract. These improvements represent millions of dollars of increased profits that show up on the bottom line every year.

If your schedule is not tailored to fit your unique needs or your concept of a new schedule is based on the simplistic notion of not increasing costs, opportunities will be lost. Best Cost Scheduling technology can boost your productivity 10 to 20 percent without adding equipment or people. Not only can you save your operation millions of dollars every year, but you can improve employee morale and health and safety.

Dispelling Misconceptions

Managers sometimes shy away from shift work because of several infamous industrial catastrophes that occurred on the night shift. Three Mile Island (4:00 A.M.), Chernobyl (1:00 A.M.), Bhopal (midnight), and Exxon *Valdez* (midnight) are the most commonly cited examples. In Chapter 3 we will find out whether shift work contributed to these accidents and how similar accidents might be prevented. Safety and health do not need to be compromised if you include the latest research knowledge into your design. One U.S. energy company had been operating 5 days a week with fixed 8-hour shifts (the employees' hours remain constant) for nearly a decade. After we worked with their managers and employees, it elected to implement a 7-day-a-week, year-round schedule with 12-hour rotating (the employees' hours change on a regular basis) shifts. In the first year of implementation, it won an award for being the safest operation in the United States in its industry.

From the employee viewpoint, the very term *shift work* usually conjures up a litany of problems. But this does not have to be the case if the schedule design is tailored to the employee desires. A television film crew once asked me to locate a 24-hour facility for a documentary titled, *Problems of Shift Work.* I directed them to a utility in San Francisco that had recently implemented a new work schedule based on Best Cost Scheduling technology. The first dozen employees the film crew interviewed stated that they preferred their current shift work lifestyle, even over day work. (In addition to thirty 3-day weekends, the new schedule provided up to 10 weeks of vacation per year.) This response continued interview after interview, until the producer decided to change the story to the benefits of working around the clock.

Other misconceptions abound concerning shift work scheduling. Most managers who are asked to consider the concept of a 24-hour business or 7-day operation think that this schedule will work only if their customer demand is peaking. This is not necessarily true. Maybe your newest, most productive, and highest quality equipment should run continuously while your other equipment is idle or is being maintained. Maybe you should run 24 hours a day but only 3 days a week to avoid start-up and shutdown costs on certain equipment. Don't let a schedule you didn't design determine how you run your business. Figure out your business needs; then design your schedule.

When it comes to shift work schedules, managers often don't identify what exactly is wrong, and then they're surprised that the answers are complex. A $500 million semiconductor plant called us in to see how good their shift-to-shift communication was, and at the end of the day we identified $75 million of lost profit opportunities due to poor capital utilization. A paint manufacturer asked us to help reduce overtime; the solution, we found, was to develop a schedule that *increased* overtime (during some months) to match a seasonal workload, while achieving an overall cost savings for the year. You may be wondering whether all of these success stories are possible, but truth is stranger than fiction.

There is no instant recipe for success. A paper mill manager asked us how he could give his employees a break from their excessive overtime without hiring more people. Their Best Cost Schedule solution was to run paper machine number 1 for 168 hours each week (thus avoiding costly shutdowns and start-ups), run paper machine 2 for 100 hours each week, and have a flexible schedule system, without any overtime.

Defining Some Terms

Before we get started, let's define a few terms. *Shift work* is work done outside normal daytime hours. We call employees who work Monday through Friday, 8:00 A.M. to 4:00 P.M., and in a department open 24 hours *day shift workers*. A *day worker* is an employee who works Monday through Friday during daylight hours and whose job is not continued into the evening. In general, this book concerns businesses that run a minimum of 60 hours a week, often 24 hours a day, and in some cases 7 days a week, or even 365 days per year. If you are already working all 8,760 hours in the year, this book will show you how to do it better. If you're considering expanding your operation, this book will show you how to do it right.

Shift work can be classified into four basic categories, depending on the workload and the need for coverage:

1. Continuous, balanced* coverage, 24 hours a day, 365 days a year, with a constant workload so that the number of workers on each shift is the same (e.g., nuclear power plants, refineries, continuous process chemical plants).
2. Continuous, unbalanced** coverage, 24 hours a day, 365 days a year, with a nonuniform workload where coverage is required beyond the daylight hour shifts, but with a different number of workers on each shift (e.g., service industries, police forces, hospitals, maintenance departments).
3. Shift coverage required by economic demand but not necessarily 24 hours a day, 7 days a week. Because the shifts can be cut back depending on the business climate, they may not be needed at certain hours, certain days of the week, or certain times of the year (e.g., manufacturing plants).
4. Irregular shift work, with occasional shift work required and scheduling that can be unpredictable (e.g., train crews, truck drivers, and some service industries).

A *model* is a system for deploying capital and personnel with a key operations concept and numerous derived schedules.

A *schedule* is one of a number of day-off patterns derived from a model, with employee buy-in and work, pay, and coverage policies tailored to that schedule.

A schedule with a 4-day weekend could be classified by Coleman Consulting Group as a 168-42, balanced, four-crew, 12-hour, fixed shift with a 4-4, or it could be classified as a 110-38.3, unbalanced, 12 crews, plus 2 supplemental crews, 10 and 8 hour, rotat-

*Same number of employees on duty at all hours.
**Different number of employees on duty at all hours.

ing, long break (the schedule shown in Figure 1-4). The first number, 168 or 110, refers to the number of hours per week the operation is running. The second number, 42 or 38.3, refers to the average number of hours per week worked by employees. This notation may seem daunting to you at this point, but in Chapter 5 we will describe and translate these terms so you will have a powerful, clear method to classify and analyze schedules.

In the past, schedules were designed primarily on tradition; contract, legal, and payroll requirements; or employee social desires. Today more and more schedules are being geared to customer demand. A 24-hour business has the advantage of flexibility and availability to meet its customer needs. Even in the continuous-process (never-put-out-the-fire) industries that have been working around the clock for years, the customer is demanding lower costs, higher quality, and better-trained operators to improve safety and lower environmental impact. These requirements can be met with better scheduling. An oil refinery, for example, can save over $2 million a year by improving its relief schedule and at the same time build in 100 hours per year for operator certification and training.

The costs of *not* going to 24-hour scheduling may be fatal: Your company may not survive to compete in a global 24-hour marketplace. If you think traditional scheduling practices will keep you competitive, you'd better hope your competition feels the same way. If your competition is lowering its costs by concentrating its efforts into one location that never shuts down, with lower equipment and labor costs, or is more productive, they will have an advantage.

The "Perfect" Schedule

What does the perfect schedule look like from the standpoint of business needs, employee desires, and health and safety requirements? If you have no vision of perfection or what you're aiming for, you are condemned to copy from others, possibly repeating their mistakes. By defining the perfect schedule, you can choose the elements that fit your situation and/or evaluate whether your current schedule is a Best Cost option. So even though you want the best shift schedule for your business now, let's look at the ideal world. I promise to come back to reality in the next five chapters.

Let's start with a clean slate. Imagine that you own a small business. There's a large market for your new product. You want to get the most out of your capital investment, so you decide to operate the business 24 hours a day, 365 days a year. Let's start designing your perfect work schedule from the business viewpoint.

Business Needs

A perfect schedule would provide the exact number of employees arriving at work every hour of the year to match the workload. If two people were needed at a given hour, two would show up; if only one were needed, only one would be there. There would be no overstaffing and no understaffing; all the work would be paid at straight time.

Furthermore, your employees would handle all the scheduling. As owner and manager of your new business, you should spend your time developing the business and making it profitable, not worrying about the employees' coverage, vacation time, or sick days. If you can trust your employees to make expensive operating decisions every night when you're not there, why not trust them to schedule their own hours of work?

To simplify matters, suppose that in your business you require only one employee at any moment in time to keep your highly automated operation going. You must make one major decision: How many people should you hire?

There are about 8,800 hours in a calendar year. If you hire four shift workers, each would have to work 2,200 hours. In comparison, the average American day worker works about 1,840 hours per year (that is, 2,080 hours—52 weeks times 40 hours per week—minus 240 hours off for holidays, personal/sick days, and vacations). Since your new shift workers will have to work holidays, weekends, and nights and maybe rotate shifts, they should probably work fewer annual hours than day workers; 1,800 hours seems about right.

Why not hire five employees and schedule each for 1,752 core (basic job coverage) hours, plus about 50 hours of *discretionary time*, when employees are assigned to develop and implement ideas to improve your business's productivity? They are called *discretionary* hours because they can be scheduled at will, as long as it happens this year. Checking with your investors, you learn that there is $200,000 in the budget for labor, including sick leave, benefits, vacations, holidays, and so forth. In that case, each shift worker would be paid a flat salary of $40,000 a year, in return for providing 1,802 annual work hours.

Once you hire your five employees, their entire employee handbook or contract would be as follows:

Provide the coverage required, and make sure you're always fit for duty. Good luck, work it out!!

There would be no specific vacations, personal days, holidays, shift differentials, weekend premium pay, or sick days. All these potential schedule busters would be built into the master schedule and salary.

Most shift work operation managers I've talked to agree that this would be an ideal around-the-clock schedule. It perfectly matches the workload, is self-scheduling, contains no overtime or idle time, provides fitness for duty, and has built-in discretionary workload coverage. In addition, guaranteed coverage for core jobs is provided every hour. Shift work is different from day work. In 24-hour shift work, coverage for the core workload is needed now. In day work, there is more of a discretionary workload. If employees are sick, on vacation, or in training classes, they can catch up later.

Of course, companies rarely operate on this kind of schedule. It's an ideal, a concept to guide us in developing better shift work operations. Most organizations have the opposite problem: They have no vision of what a good shift schedule would be. No one at the facility knows who designed the schedule or what the key concept is behind the design. The schedule may not even come close to matching the organization's workload. In one case, a utility had 100 employees come to work on Wednesdays but only 60 on Mondays. No more electricity was being produced on Wednesdays than on Mondays; the utility's work schedule simply did not match its workload. This error (though in smaller scale) is more common than you might imagine. Many businesses don't realize they are frequently understaffed or overstaffed, even overmatching and undermatching the workload in the same week.

Employee Desires

Now that we've looked at the perfect schedule from the view of business needs, let's turn to employee desires. Shift workers' ideal schedule (excluding staying home and receiving a paycheck) would be something like this: They would work Monday through Thursday, spending 8 hours a day at work. During those 8 hours, employees would be paid for a 1-hour lunch and two half-hour breaks. In addition, they would be paid for the 1-hour commute time getting to work and 1 hour getting home. Forty pay hours are reached in 4 days, even though only 24 hours of actual work is being done. Friday, Saturday, and Sunday would all be overtime, paid at triple-time rates. The employees would have the option of working these days or staying home. Of course, your business would shut down on nights and holidays; in fact, it would have to close the day before holidays (to prepare) and the day after (to recover). There would be a mid-year shutdown as well as a Christmas shutdown. Basically, shift workers' perfect schedule is to get a schedule as close to a day worker's as possible—perhaps even better than a day worker's—but to receive the pay and benefits of shift work.

Health and Safety Requirements

It's also possible to have the perfect schedule for the health and safety circle. If your only goal was to have employees alert at 3:00 A.M., I would recommend a schedule something like this: Have employees work 365 consecutive night shifts in a row, with the night shift starting at 1:00 A.M. and ending at 5:00 A.M. At work there would be bright lights to simulate sunlight in order to reset the biological clock and exercise stations to help overcome any bouts of sleepiness that might occur. At 5:00 A.M. the employees would go home on a darkened bus. Their homes would be located in a quiet environment, perhaps a special shift worker housing complex outside of town. Their rooms would be air-conditioned, sound- and light-proofed, and therefore totally dark. The shift workers would have no family or other social life, so they could religiously obtain 9 hours of sleep each day.

From a strictly biological clock viewpoint, this schedule would be very healthy—healthier than day workers'. You might think this inversion of the body's physiology would not promote good health; nevertheless, remember that while you are reading this book, most people halfway across the world are sleeping. If you were to move to Russia, within a week your body physiology would invert 180 degrees to fit that country's sleep/wake schedules. Similarly, shift workers could make a complete adjustment if they worked this idealized schedule. The reason I scheduled 365 consecutive nights was to stay in rhythm. Any days off would be likely to have the night workers revert to a normal day routine. Finally, our shift workers are getting plenty of sleep—9 hours a day—and the 4-hour shift length would be compatible with most work tasks.

The Proper Balance

In practice, there is no such thing as a purely perfect schedule. Designing shift schedules is a balancing act. No operation will always match the workload, some shift workers will have to work on Christmas, and not every employee will be alert at every hour. In the real world of scheduling, you need to blend and balance the three key schedule design elements to find the Best Cost Schedule for your site.

In many businesses, these three circles are not properly balanced. For example, at one oil refinery, management had a policy that required employees to stand by on their days off in case someone got sick in the middle of the shift. This schedule is fantastic for the business circle, ensuring coverage even in the rare case of a shift worker's becoming ill at the refinery in the middle of the shift, but disastrous for the employee circle. Shift workers could never fully enjoy a day off knowing they could be called in at any time. Ultimately the schedule failed. Other schedules are weighted too heavily to the employee circle. A manufacturer in Australia had so many rostered (scheduled) days off—public holidays, vacation days, weekends, vacation shutdowns, picnic day, and others—that the plant was open fewer than 200 days a year. The corporate managers considered investing new capital for new export markets, but this plant was low on the list unless it increased its operating schedule. Ultimately, job security was worse for these shift workers until they changed schedules.

At Coleman Consulting Group, our expertise is really in two areas: (1) finding the proper balance and designing the Best Cost Schedule options for a specific business from the thousands of possibilities and (2) finding a successful way to implement that schedule at a given location. By constantly talking to shift work managers and shift workers in different industries, countries, and situations, we have learned that 24-hour work schedules can be continually improved. Tremendous benefits accrue from implementing Best Cost Schedules; if done properly, the change process and its result will be a positive experience for employees, their families, managers, employers, and stockholders.

Many of the readers of this book are also experts in shift work. However, most will be an expert only on the one schedule at their business. If you are a manager, you have become an expert at figuring out how to operate under your head count constraints while meeting customer needs and holding the lid on overtime. If you are a first-line supervisor, you've learned how to stretch your resources to the maximum to keep product going out the door while still trying to meet the individual time-off needs of your crew members. If you are a shift worker, you are probably an expert on pay policies—how to obtain more overtime or avoid it altogether—and how to maximize your chance of getting onto the best shift. If you are the spouse or family member of a shift worker, you have become an expert on how to manage your life around the shift schedule. One of the reasons it's so hard to change schedules is that everyone has become an expert with the current system, even if the fundamental schedule is the wrong one.

I realize you might be thinking that your situation is different. That's probably true. However, throughout this book we will hear from managers, shift workers, their family members, and union leaders with different problems and solutions. I think you'll find the problems you face are more alike than they are different. We will follow one person in particular. His name is Richard Scallan ("Dick" to his friends), and he is the general manager of Australia's largest tin mine for Renison Limited in Tasmania. Scallan has worked for various companies, mainly in Australia and Africa, in underground and surface mines, including gold, nickel, copper, chrome, and tin. As a mine manager, he says, "The first and foremost thing is to make a profit and continue to make a profit, and be as cost-effective as possible. I have been at the Tasmania site for three years. When I came in, it had just gone through a very severe restructuring. It was totally unprofitable and had lost about $13 million the previous year. There was a lot of heartache, a lot of strife, a lot of employee disruption, and the undercurrents were at work. The mine was very close to going out of business. We had restructured but were extremely vulnerable, and the price of tin was low. I had to get the mine productive. I had to change things."

In Chapter 2 we will look at what Scallan changed, concentrating on the business needs circle at his company, Renison, as well as at your business.

2

Business Needs

If you have the right equipment and the right employees, at the right place, at the right time, at the right cost, you have the perfect business schedule. If you're close to this ideal, skip this chapter. Otherwise, read on. If you're like most businesses, you can probably improve your schedule, improvements that reach all the way to the bottom line. And unlike adding employees, materials, or capital equipment, better scheduling is a cost-free way to improve profitability. A good schedule can save you millions. A bad schedule will cost you money.

Since you are still reading this chapter, you clearly believe there's a better way to schedule. Now what? Suppose you were asked to design a 24-hour schedule for your business.

Getting Started

Your first instinct might be to copy a schedule from a neighboring plant or a competitor, or maybe ask your employees what they prefer. In this manner, you could develop a new schedule in a few hours, but it probably would not fit your business needs. Just as you do not employ exactly the same technology, equipment, or sales strategy as another company, some other company's schedule is not likely to be right for you. A work schedule has a dramatic impact on capital costs, ability to meet customer needs, and productivity. With the right schedule, you can be a low-cost, high-quality producer. If the schedule is wrong, you will have a host of problems.

Actually the impulse to start by selecting a schedule is wrong.

Instead, start by determining your business needs. Then find a schedule model that provides the best fit.

In Chapter 1, Dick Scallan described the precarious situations he faced when he was hired at Renison Gold Consolidated Limited. I asked him, "When you looked at all the possible things to change at your mine, what were your first key targets?" Here is his reply:

> The plant was working a 5-day roster [schedule], or Monday through Friday, even though it had been designed for continuous operations. We spent most of our time starting it up and then shutting it down. There was no opportunity for maintenance, an unacceptable situation, so we had to get the plant running continuously.
>
> But this was just dealing with the availability of the plant. More important, we had to get the ore to the plant from the underground mine. That's where I saw the greatest need for change—and the greatest resistance to change. The mine had traditionally worked 80 hours a week (two 40-hour shifts). When the effectiveness of this schedule was analyzed, we found out we were probably only getting 4.5 effective hours out of every 8 hours worked. People were either waiting or having to travel tremendous distances before they got to their workplace, and they couldn't understand why they had to hang around and be so unproductive.
>
> The mine was getting progressively deeper, and as these distances increased, costs went spiraling up. We were putting in more equipment and more people, but becoming less productive. I had to change the schedule, an enormous challenge because of the resistance to change. But the change was critical to keeping the mine open. I knew I would have only one chance to do this, and I had to get it right.

Defining the Workload

The first step in finding your Best Cost Schedule is to define the workload, not a simple task. The workload may vary from hour to hour, day to day, week to week, season to season or from department to department or job to job. Workloads may be as simple to measure as, "We need one security guard on duty every hour of the year," or as complex as, "We manufacture and ship over 300 different customer products, and our customer orders come in at the last minute." Companies that do not routinely measure their workload practice backward scheduling, fitting the workload into their current schedule even though that schedule may be the wrong one. The result is often a big gap between the master schedule (the one that's posted in the employee handbook or printed in the union contract) and the actual schedule (the one that is really worked). Many companies become experts at backward scheduling and are able to stretch their master schedule to the limits, keeping customers satisfied, but the negative impact on productivity, safety, overtime, and morale can cost millions of dollars every year.

Businesses can run 24 hours for different reasons—some because customers demand it (police, fire, hospitals, supermarkets), some because it's the most economical option, and others because the process requires it. Even in continuous never-put-out-the-fire operations, such as a refinery, steel mill, or power plant, the workload is often not scrutinized carefully enough, with the assumption that the same number of people are required at all hours. This *balanced staffing* is represented by the dotted line in Figure 2-1.

Daily and Weekly Workload

In practice the workload may fluctuate slightly every day. Often there is a larger workload on the day shift, slightly less on the evening shift, and significantly less on the night shift. Many shift workers in continuous operations complain about the stress of the day shift; there are "too many cars in the parking lot," meaning the presence of managers, maintenance workers, engineers, and technicians. Product changes are often done on the day shift and so the workload is higher then than on the "back shifts"—afternoons, nights, weekends, and holidays—which are often slightly overstaffed. In addition, many petrochemical and utility plants build in relief workers on each crew for sickness, vacation, and training coverage. But what happens at 3:00 A.M. on a Sunday in January if

Figure 2-1. Defining the daily workload.

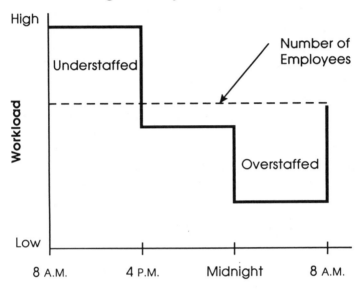

no one is sick or on vacation? The regular crew, along with the relief workers, show up, but effective training won't take place at this hour, so employees are idle.

In manufacturing plants with 5-day-a-week operations, the workload issues usually concern overtime and maintenance. Many manufacturers concentrate their production Monday through Friday, 24 hours per day, with some Saturday overtime. The bulk of maintenance workers, however, are scheduled during the Monday through Friday day shifts, the very hours when production is fully loaded. As a result, maintenance workers are not utilized efficiently during weekdays and then preventive maintenance is fitted on weekends using overtime and reduced maintenance crews. Figure 2-2 shows one method for matching a 5-day workload in order to maximize production while building in corrective and preventive maintenance.

Obviously, there are unlimited numbers of workload scenarios and Figures 2-1 and 2-2 are not illustrative of all businesses. Nevertheless, it is instructive to graph and analyze your own workload. To do so, look at last year's total production or customer service by time. Determine what the ideal deployment of personnel

**Figure 2-2. Ideal operations/maintenance scheduling—
5-day work schedule.**

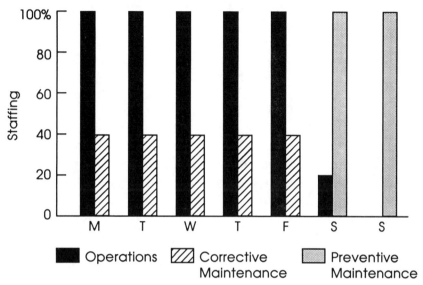

would have been by time to accomplish this level of productivity. Compare it with your actual manning. Then divide the theoretical hours needed by the actual hours utilized to get your schedule efficiency index. Pacesetters run around 90 percent efficiency.

When you sketch your workload, assume you have an unlimited supply of employees from another planet who will work any hours for free and don't need sleep. In other words, don't be limited initially by what you think employees like or dislike or by what's in your union contract or current practices. For starters, try to describe your workload based on your customer demand or lowest cost use of capital and labor. If you start by assuming what employees will like or dislike, you may end up with "day work mentality" syndrome, which can cost your business millions of dollars.

One of the worst mistakes large manufacturers make is to add plants and equipment when their original investments are insufficiently utilized. In 1994 the majority of manufacturing clients we contacted were running their plants below 50 percent of available hours. An automotive component parts plant operating at 37 percent of possible hours is typical. General Motors, Chrysler, and Ford are now considering consolidating plants and running continuously. Remember, there are 8,760 hours in a year. The maximum capital utilization for a plant running three full shifts, 5 days a week, is only 71 percent. If the equipment is up 85 percent of the time and holidays, vacation, lunch, and breaks are taken into consideration, usage is closer to 47 percent. That means capital equipment is idle at least half the year. Why not get your first plant or piece of equipment running more hours before you purchase your second?

The number of operating hours in a day ranges from 0 to 24, and in a week from 0 to 168. Separate the hours needed to run your operation from the number of hours an individual must work. Once an operating schedule is set, a shift schedule for employees can be developed. One business may run 152 hours a week, with each shift worker averaging a 40-hour workweek (this is called a "152-40"), while another business runs 80 hours a week with each shift worker averaging a 46-hour workweek (an "80-46"). If your operating schedule is 120 hours with three 40-hour crews (a "120-40"), be skeptical. It's too great a coincidence that customer demand for your product comes out to exactly 120 hours of production. Maybe you need 114.6 hours a week, or 137 hours a week, or maybe even 92 hours during one quarter and 160 in another quarter. Is your operating schedule truly what your business requires, or is it just a convenient fit with overtime law, contract, tradition, or simplicity? Base your operating schedule on the most effective use of your capital equipment, the most effective regular maintenance schedule, and your customer demand.

Yearly Workload

In addition to evaluating your daily and weekly workload, determine your yearly workload too. Figure 2-3 shows the annual workload for a Queensland, Australia, mining operation that needed exactly 1,480 man-hours every week of the year to meet its customer demand (represented by the solid horizontal line).

The graph shows that despite the need for a constant manning

Figure 2-3. Annual workload analysis for a mining operation.

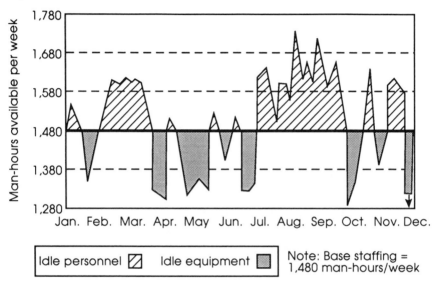

level, in practice this company's man-hours are always either above the line, reaching close to 1,750 hours during August and September (winter in Australia, when vacation leave is low), or below the line, with only 1,280 hours in December (summer, when leave is high). The area above the line represents idle labor time when more employees come to work than are needed. Idle labor time is very expensive. One hour of idle time typically has ten times greater adverse cost effect on your business than 1 hour of overtime. The labor cost of mismatching the workload at this one mine is $2.5 million per year. Below the line represents idle equipment, which is also very expensive (a truck/shovel/dragline operation will easily cost $100 million to $200 million). More efficient schedules can reduce capital outlays. Mismatch of such predictable, balanced workloads may be due to vacation policy, sickness policy, overtime rules, holidays, training, scheduling policies, preventive maintenance scheduling, and other inefficiencies.

When planning your yearly schedule, stick to your business needs. Many companies have a summer shutdown for 2 weeks and another at Christmas that they say is for required maintenance.

But closer inspection reveals that the shutdown is really to meet employee desires. A 14-day maintenance shutdown may actually require only 3 days. Unless equipment must be shut down for maintenance, a summer, Christmas, or holiday shutdown is not recommended; avoiding these shutdowns can increase plant utilization by 7 percent (more profits without adding equipment or people). In fact, shift schedules exist that make working holidays attractive. In one schedule model, employees who elect to work 8 holidays during the year can receive an extra 28-day paid break during the summer without using vacation leave in exchange.

Seasonal Workload

Businesses with consistent peak seasons and slack periods have predictable, seasonal workloads. All of the candy makers we have worked with have a tremendous peak before October, when there is a huge increase in candy purchases because of Halloween. Some seasonal workloads occur for less obvious reasons. A maker of furnaces for the glass industry has a peak workload in the fourth quarter. Its customers try to avoid ordering furnace upgrades and often end up making a decision toward the very end of the fiscal year. Of course, then the customer wants that new furnace right away.

Proper scheduling of seasonal workloads depends on matching a series of complex variables. Is outsourcing an option? Should the company buy enough equipment and employ enough shift workers to match production during the peak quarter, or should it have less equipment in place and build up inventory? What is the cost of carrying this inventory? Most American manufacturers today are trying to keep inventory costs down, using just-in-time manufacturing. This strategy would argue for having equipment in place for the peak loads, especially if equipment is not costly. However, if capital equipment is very expensive, building up inventory could be cheaper. Some facilities we visit have developed expertise at maintaining low inventory, but their plants are loaded with millions of dollars worth of capital equipment that is sitting idle much of the year.

There are a variety of tools you can use to match a seasonal workload:

- Decrease/increase overtime.
- Build up/draw down inventory.
- Schedule/limit time off.
- Lay off/add temporaries and part-time employees.
- Lay off/add full-time employees.
- Revise shift schedules.

Here are four systems to match changing seasonal workloads:

1. *Provide incentives for employees to take vacation time when the workload is low.* Some schedules do not allow employees to take actual vacation time during peak work periods in the summer, yet each employee, no matter how junior, receives a week off in June, a week off in July, and a week off in August. How? The schedule does it. The schedule has a built-in week off without using vacation hours.
2. *Change the shift lengths.* A manufacturer with a 7-day seasonal workload never forced employees to come in on their days off but expanded their 10-hour shifts to 12-hour shifts during the peak times. This allowed for more overall production hours without disrupting the employees' days off.
3. *Have different operating schedules that don't require hiring or firing employees or using extensive overtime.* At one of the Lever Brothers newer plants, there are three different shift schedules, each without overtime, for 5-day, 6-day, and 7-day coverage.
4. *Have a weekly layoff plan.* Management has the right to lay off employees each week depending on customer demand. This is an excellent system to reduce idle time and match the workload but may have a costly negative side of poor morale, constant bidding out, and breaking up of crews, since layoffs are typically based on a seniority system.

Unpredictable Workload

Maybe you're thinking, "Hey, my workload is unpredictable." You're not alone. In Illinois, Moore Business Services, printer of magazines and direct mail, often doesn't receive customers' orders until Friday afternoon, when a flood of faxes and express packages arrives for next week's run. Management must decide on Friday how much weekend work is needed and how to turn around customers' orders. However, Moore's seemingly impossible, unpredictable workload still has an average demand and typical variations. Although a workload may be unpredictable when you focus on one particular day (what will happen on the thirty-eighth Saturday of this year?), if you stand back and look at a larger period of time, you may find the variance is predictable.

Employees at the headquarters marketing desk of a chain of retail service stations answer telephones whenever a customer has a credit card problem. Since their service stations are open 24 hours a day and are located from the East Coast to Hawaii, the phones must be covered every hour of the year. Developing the correct schedule for the employees who handle these calls (and who are based in California) began by analyzing the frequency of phone calls by the time of day and day of the year. The resulting schedule (Figure 2-4), which involved eighteen crews, had more employees on day shift than on afternoon, more on afternoon than night, more on weekday nights than weekend nights, and so on. In addition, special floater shifts were built into the schedule to be flexible with handling unpredictable workload swings. The key in service industries is to anticipate customers' regular needs while being prepared for unexpected fluctuations.

Unbalanced Workload

Even if the workload is predictable and steady, it may be unbalanced. Different numbers of employees may be required at different times of the day, week, or year. Hospitals typically run with unbalanced workloads, with more coverage during weekdays and less on nights and weekends. Is this due to an unbalanced workload or employee convenience? Many patients would understandably prefer to see their doctors on evenings and weekends, and this would also improve utilization of expensive medical machines that are idle most of each 24-hour period. If you have an unbalanced workload, analyze whether it is based on your best business needs (low capital costs and meeting customer demand) or not, and if so, take advantage of it with an unbalanced schedule.

Figure 2-4. Schedule for a customer service provider with an unpredictable workload (168–40, unbalanced, 18-crew, 8 + 12-hour, rotating, primary, 5-2).

Crew	M	T	W	T	F	S	S
1	N	d	d	d	d	-	-
2	d	d	d	d	d	-	-
3	d	d	d	d	d	-	-
4	d	d	d	d	d	-	-
5	d	d	d	d	d	-	-
6	d	d	d	d	d	-	-
7	-	-	-	f	f	D	D
8	d	-	f	f	-	D	D
9	f	f	-	-	-	D	D
10	a	a	a	a	a	-	-
11	a	a	a	a	a	-	-
12	a	a	a	a	a	-	-
13	a	a	a	a	a	-	-
14	-	n	n	n	n	N	-
15	-	n	n	n	n	N	-
16	-	n	n	n	n	N	-
17	-	-	f	f	-	-	N
18	N	f	f	-	-	-	N

n = 8-hour night shift   = 10 P.M.–6 A.M.
d = 8-hour day shift   = 6 A.M.–2 P.M.
a = 8-hour afternoon shift = 2 P.M.–10 P.M.
f = 8-hour flexible shift = varying hours
N = 12-hour night shift   = 6 P.M.–6 A.M.
D = 12-hour day shift   = 6 A.M.–6 P.M.
- = off
Night shift is first shift of the day (starts night before).
Work week starts at 6 A.M. on Monday.

Other companies have a workload that is inverse. For instance, their transactions may occur during the day, but their computer systems process them at night. Such companies need more people on the night shift than on the day shift. Credit card companies, financial institutions, and stock brokerages are examples of businesses that may have inverse workloads.

Discretionary Workload

When you analyze your work requirements, remember to define both your *core* workload (coverage for the basic jobs) and *discretionary* workload (tasks that must be completed this year but on a flexible schedule—for example, training, team meetings, material handling, clean-up, and interaction with maintenance, laboratory, customers, and suppliers). Many companies are moving to self-directed work teams whereby diverse teams of workers meet to develop and implement productivity improvements. Some companies want their shift workers to meet with customers and suppliers and handle their own administration, or best of all, to spend part of their working year thinking about how to reduce costs and improve productivity.

If time is not built into the master schedule for discretionary workload, these activities become "schedule busters"—liabilities instead of assets—causing expense (overtime) and disrupting employees' time off. Most companies faced with choosing discretionary workload or meeting customer demand choose the customer and stop discretionary work. As a result, continuous improvement is talked about but does not actually happen because it's not built into the regular yearly work schedule.

Factoring in Idle Labor Time and Overtime

Without a careful understanding of idle time and overtime hours, it is nearly impossible to develop a Best Cost Schedule.

Idle Labor Time

Imagine you have an entire crew of shift workers who are being paid full wages and benefits and are working very hard for 8 hours. You need to have the entire crew stay over for the ninth hour to meet an extra customer shipment. Although you are paying time and a half (premium), you have already paid the majority of the employees' benefits in the first 8 hours, so the ninth hour is productive and relatively cheap. On the other hand, if the entire crew is standing around for an hour during their regular 8-hour shift waiting for maintenance to repair a piece of equipment, they are still receiving full pay and benefits but doing no work. This is unproductive and expensive.

Idle labor time—the cost of overmatching the workload—is more expensive than overtime, but few companies generate an idle time report, even though the payback could be ten times greater. Because idle time is harder to measure than overtime, it often is neglected. A manufacturer in Kentucky with ninety employees asked us to reduce weekend overtime, which was costing about $280,000 a year. We found that idle labor time in this plant was actually costing over $1,000,000 a year! By changing the work schedule and policies, idle labor time can be significantly reduced, but you need to measure it before you can fix it.

The worst situation is to have both idle time and overtime in the same week. Many companies have high idle time Monday through Friday and then schedule overtime on the weekend to catch up on work that did not get completed. This is very common in maintenance departments in manufacturing plants. Furthermore, scheduling policies and pay practices may have incentives for the buildup of idle time and subsequent overtime. At an auto parts manufacturer in Illinois, idle time during the Monday through Friday workweek was over 20 percent; weekend overtime to catch up was nearly 25 percent, in a classic lose-lose situation for management.

Overtime

Overtime is supposed to be a strategic reserve of labor to be utilized for short-term workload increases. In the real world, overtime usage is rarely strategic. Ideally, overtime should go down to zero several pay periods each year, so employees and management do not become dependent on it. When overtime is consistently high, employees may become dependent on it as a source of their regular pay. They might buy another car, a boat, or a house and rely on overtime to meet their fixed payments. When management becomes more efficient—and that day always comes—overtime is cut, with a dramatically negative impact on the same employees that management want to join their team effort. Remember: A big cut in overtime may be perceived as a cut in job security.

The appropriate level of overtime is determined by wages, benefit costs, equipment costs, ratio of labor costs to product costs, and other factors. Many shift work operations in the United States (where the standard workweek is 40 hours) schedule a 42-hour workweek. This is not done through a systematic analysis but simply because 168 hours a week, divided by 4 (employees), averages 42 hours. Using RDOs, a "rostered-days-off" system common in countries like Australia, any average workweek can be established.

The most efficient level of overtime varies in different situations. Managers are sometimes proud to tell us that they are running with virtually no overtime. An oil refinery manager in Oklahoma once told us that he had "zero overtime." He even challenged us to review his books. We did, and it was true. He was 75 percent overstaffed, but had "zero overtime." If you have no overtime, then there's a high probability you're overstaffed or have high idle time—or both.

Overtime Pay

Overtime pay (mandated by federal or state government, or union contract for working extended hours) can have a critical impact on the costs of running a 7-day business, especially if your old policies were based on a 5-day-a-week operation. In the United States, the Fair Labor Standards Act requires overtime be paid to nonexempt workers for working more than 40 hours in a workweek. Furthermore, a set workweek must be maintained. You cannot change the start day and hour of the workweek every week or average overtime in a cycle. In many countries outside the U.S., both union and nonunion workers can average overtime over a cycle: An employee could work 32 hours one week and 48 hours the next week, and since the employee averaged 40 hours in that 2-week cycle, no overtime occurred. Businesses can more readily design and implement flexible schedules in these nations.

In the United States paying overtime to employees after they work 8 hours in a 24-hour period is not a federal requirement, but it is a requirement of some states, industries, and/or union contracts. And there is an array of exceptions and special circumstances, such as in California, where overtime is required after 8 hours except in certain industries when two-thirds of the employees agree to waive this provision in order to work extended shift lengths.

Premium Pay

A distinction should be made between overtime pay and *premium pay*, defined as extra pay linked to specific days or hours (double time for Sunday, double time for holidays, fifty cents more per hour for night work, an extra 5 percent for working rotating shifts, etc.). Premium pay is usually the result of a union contract or industry practice or even state law, but it is not part of the U.S. federal overtime law.

Paying a premium to make up for a bad schedule is a concept we call *bribes accepted*. The rationale is that these plants are paying a penalty for the injustice of forcing unattractive schedules on their workforce (weekends) and/or it's assumed that anyone working Saturday or Sunday has already put in his or her 40 hours that week. These are expensive, erroneous assumptions.

The more that management bribes employees to work shift work, the greater is the chance of poor morale, or the "stuck in shift work" syndrome. At Queensland Electricity Commission, a utility in Australia, a rotating shift worker can earn about $70,000 a year, whereas a day worker makes closer to $35,000 a year. The rotating shift workers hate their schedule and morale is low, but when asked, "Why don't you bid out and go into day work?" their answer is obvious: "I can't, because my wages would be cut in half." Because of shift premiums a plant manager at another Australian facility complained that he was the thirty-ninth highest paid employee in his seventy-person operation.

The record we've seen for the most premiums paid for shift work was at Tasman Pulp & Paper in New Zealand, with more than 200 different items listed for working shift work, each ranging in annual costs to management from $3.9 million to 26 cents, all of which must be maintained and recorded every year, taking hundreds of man-hours to decipher, with multiple grievances to resolve disputes. Working with management, the union, and the workforce at Tasman, we helped develop a new enterprise bargaining agreement with an annual salary package, implemented along with the new schedule. Now there are no premiums for shift work, just a flat salary for working a specific number of annual hours.

If you have a bad work schedule, don't look to bribes to fix it. Instead, improve the schedule. If you don't have enough weekends off, for example, develop a schedule that has more weekends off. If pay is unfair, work that out as a separate issue. However, different schedules will require different pay policies to avoid "take aways" from employees and cost overruns for management. In Chapter 6, we will discuss whether it is possible to convert these policies without upsetting your workforce.

Why Seven-Day Schedules?

If you are considering maximizing your resources, you will need to run 365 days a year, 24 hours a day. In the past, only companies where the process could never be stopped or shut down ran these schedules. Now all sorts of businesses are running 7 full days.

There are six major reasons that companies (excluding those that are continuous process and start out 7-day) choose to change to 7-day schedules:

1. *To defer capital expenditures.* (Usually for equipment, but sometimes for space. A semiconductor plant in Texas needed to increase output to meet a significant increase in demand. By running equipment more efficiently and for more hours, it was able to defer a $50 million investment and decreased the need to outsource, saving $75 million over a 5-year period.

2. *To produce more with current capital.* Companies in the electronics industry may hit on a hot product with a short life span and need to jump to a 7-day workweek while customer demand is peaking. Other manufacturers find they can increase profit margins by operating more hours with the same capital equipment, where in the past the sales force may have been told "we're at capacity" or the company had been letting another company handle some production needs (outsourcing). It pays to have a 7-day-a-week solution ready to implement so you don't limit your sales potential.

3. *To consolidate current capital.* Ralston Purina, headquartered in St. Louis, had an opportunity to lower fixed costs by shutting down a plant and moving the work to other plants. Two existing plants had to expand to 7-day-a-week operations to accommodate the extra production. In another case, a tire manufacturer with multiple sites found it could save over $10 million annually by moving production from sister plants to the plant with lower production costs. The low-cost plant would need a 7-day-a-week schedule to take on the extra manufacturing.

4. *To eliminate costly weekend start-ups and shutdowns.* Productivity often falls in anticipation of a shutdown and may remain low several hours into start-up. Working through the weekends could save millions in start-up and shutdown costs. Waste, poor use of materials, low yields, and quality errors can be part of each of these events. If you can't just switch on a button Monday morning and resume maximum productivity and quality immediately, maybe you should run your equipment through the weekend.

5. *To reduce overtime pay and/or excessive overtime.* If employees on a 5-day master schedule are working numerous weekends, chances are you are paying premium wages just when your shift workers are at their most exhausted and likely to make a quality or operating error. Many companies consider changing schedules only when they are in this crisis mode, having missed earlier opportunities.

6. *To make use of what we call BEST™,* for Best Equipment STrategy. This is a scheduling system where your most productive equipment is scheduled 7 days a week, even when the overall production demand for *all* your capital is well below a 7-day require-

ment. (See Figure 2-5.) Even in a recession or low workload situation, it may make sense to operate 7 days a week, using your BEST equipment full-out and holding the remainder offline for preventive maintenance. The Best Equipment STrategy allows you to run your best (latest, fastest, higher quality) equipment all week, increasing productivity and quality. Older, less productive equipment can go offline and be rotated into service as needed.

There are other applications for 7-day-a-week schedules as well, such as developing and introducing a new product to the marketplace more quickly by turning marketing or engineering teams into temporary 24-hour operations, reducing customer lead time, deferring the need for extra space, or simply matching customer demand for 7-day coverage. More and more companies are moving to 7-day-a-week operations to increase capital utilization, operate more efficiently, and be more profitable. Although such a schedule may sound negative to employees initially, plants that implement one offer the best job security because they become low-cost, fully utilized producers. Many 7-day schedules provide attractive time off and foster a healthier lifestyle than 5-day schedules. Some 7-day-a-week schedules double days off, increase 2-day weekends to 3-day weekends, while adding weeks of vacation and build in overtime, which should combat any perceived negative. (See Chapters 4 and 5.)

Kathleen Amrhein is the human resources manager for the bulk Chemical Division of The Upjohn Company, a pharmaceutical company located in Kalamazoo, Michigan. I asked Kathy why her company called us when she was considering a schedule change. This is her reply:

We were running full staff Monday through Friday, and half staff Saturday and Sunday, so we were a 5-day operation working lots of overtime. The shift workers were working 12 consecutive days with 2 days off. Even working that schedule we weren't able to achieve the production levels we were looking for. The excessive overtime was causing burnout, and people weren't able to plan

Figure 2-5. Using Best Equipment STrategy™.

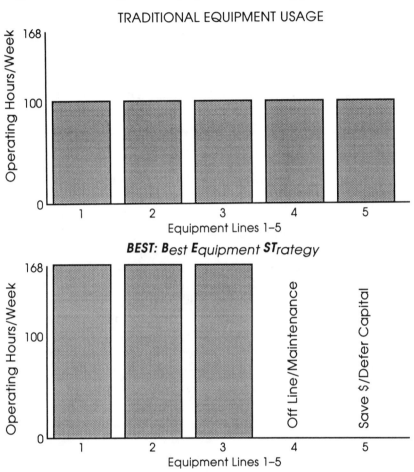

With the *Best Equipment STrategy*, quality, productivity, and preventive maintenance increase, while costs and waste decrease.

family activities because they never knew if they would have to work.

We looked at our forecast for production over the next 5 years and decided it was just not cost-effective to continue to build new production facilities. So we realized we had to run 7 days a week, 24 hours a day to meet the projected forecast. This would be a big culture change for our operators. We had to figure out how to keep them happy and interested in their jobs and yet get out the product that we need to continue in our business.

The main thing in this type of change program is to facilitate it and then keep it on track. The management team was committed to making the change, but our operators had mixed feelings. We had to look at our pay practices and see if we could reduce costs, change premium pay, and still find the most effective schedule for the company. Another hurdle was getting the employees to understand that going back to the Monday–Friday workweek was not an option.

The family education sessions that we had with the operators and their families were important. A lot of families and spouses didn't understand what shift work is all about; they didn't know about circadian rhythms and body temperature and why people can be grumpy or have more gastric problems. I think it was an awakening for a lot of family members that there are actual physiological reasons for behavior. But showing them a willingness to work at it and make some lifestyle changes to control these factors was very positively received.

We have several new schedules, and we've had very positive results. In the first 9 months of the new schedules, our spills decreased 50 percent and value added per operator went up 24.5 percent. That's our efficiency measure. The number of kilograms produced went up 19.7 percent. The number of lots that had to be reprocessed in one of the areas went down 65 percent. Our lost-time accidents decreased by 14 percent.

The biggest thing I learned is to be consistent on the messages sent and tie them into our business needs. We were asking employees to make some major lifestyle changes. We had to provide support and help them overcome any difficulties. Providing a change strategy and schedule options in terms that our employees understood made it possible to implement the change.

Before Going to 7 Days, Fix Monday!

In our consulting practice, we have stopped companies from going to 7-day operations just as often as we have recommended 7-day/week operations. Don't just put in 7-day schedules in every department. One Australian fabric manufacturer is struggling to meet customer orders and is extending shift work to cover Saturday and Sunday, and both days require paying double time. But they are getting only 20 hours of production on each weekday due to shift changes, breaks, lunches, and wash time where equipment is left idle. Instead of going to a 7-day schedule, this manufacturer would do better to get a full 24 hours of production, Monday through Friday.

Figure 2-6 shows a manufacturing plant that was, by its definition, running 5 days a week, 24 hours a day, or 120 hours per week. However, our analysis revealed that because of how it dealt with absenteeism, such as vacations, holidays, training, and shift changes, the average equipment downtime was 35.9 hours per week. If it expanded the current 24-hour-a-day schedule to 7 days a week, which was their intention, it would have *increased* the scheduled equipment downtime to 48.3 hours a week.

If you are considering a 6-day or 7-day operation, first make sure you are truly getting 24 hours of operating time Monday through Friday. Maybe you really need an efficient 4-day-a-week operation. In our business we say "Fix Mondays First" before you expand to the weekend!

The discrepancy between potential (available) and actual operating hours is related by many variables, including scheduling of breaks, lunches, shift changes, maintenance, absenteeism, training, weekend start-up and shutdowns, and skill balance. And of course, scheduled equipment also breaks down on its own. It is beneficial to analyze in detail each variable that causes downtime so you will know what to fix. Establishing a better schedule will normally cost nothing, whereas equipment upgrades can be expensive.

Staffing a 24-Hour Business

Your engineering team can calculate your ideal staffing ratio by considering benefit loading costs (cost of fringe benefits), exempt

Figure 2-6. Fixing Mondays first.

Opportunity	Average Equipment Downtime (*Hours per Week*)	
	Current Schedule	168-Hour Schedule
Breaks	9.0	10.5
Absenteeism	8.1	11.3
Vacation	5.1	7.1
Holidays	4.6	4.6
Training	4.5	6.3
Shift Change	3.0	3.5
Meetings	0.7	0.7
Other	0.9	0.9
Maintenance	0	3.4
Total (Hours)	35.9	48.3

versus nonexempt status, number of hours in the standard work-week in your locality, core and discretionary workload, relief coverage, and number of hours of availability per employee (annual straight time hours minus vacations, sick leave, and holidays). What actually takes place in operations may be quite different from the ideal. For example, a large Japanese manufacturer of personal items such as soap uses tons per employee as opposed to tons per man-hour as its key productivity measure. As a result, one of their plants has very lean staffing but high overtime and a large number of temporaries who don't count as "employees."

At an East Coast pharmaceutical manufacturer, 10 employees

are scheduled to cover a shift. During 4 hours of each 8-hour shift, there will be 5 employees at the equipment, and for the other 4 hours, all ten. What's the correct number of employees? Obviously, the facility is either tremendously overstaffed or understaffed for half the day. No one is sure which because management has not defined a core workload or minimum required staffing load. Scheduling systems that emphasize maintaining an exact minimum manning level (we call this *bare metal staffing*) force management discipline and practices that avoid routine over- and understaffing. In many operations this system is lacking. "Running short" is a standard procedure, and the results are expensive.

For most companies the number of employees covering one balanced position for 8,760 hours will range from three employees per position (a staffing ratio of 3:1) to six employees per position (6:1). However, a staffing ratio of between 4.5:1 or 5:1 is most common, in order to provide for vacancy coverage. Remember, we're talking about the actual staffing, not what the master schedule shows. A continuous chemical plant in Louisiana with a four-crew schedule and 4:1 staffing ratio on its master schedule actually had a 5:1 ratio when relief personnel were included. When I pointed this out to the plant manager, he explained, "I keep them hidden on the back shifts; I may need this manpower in the future." At Pennsylvania Power & Light's security department, where the discretionary workload was significant, a five-crew schedule with an exact 5:1 staffing ratio was a good fit. It is possible to have any staffing ratio you want; just don't confuse your crew structure with your staffing ratio. Many companies don't have a staffing ratio that management can readily quote, and this invariably results in a high cost schedule with routine over- and understaffing.

If your master schedule is a 120-40 (24 hours, 5 days a week, with each employee working 40 hours a week) with a 3:1 staffing ratio, but your actual workload including overtime is closer to 7 days, consider adding employees. The cost of three employees (salary and benefits) working 56 hours a week is equal to the cost of four employees (salary and benefits) working 42 hours a week, if you pay time and one-half on Saturday and double time on Sunday. Nevertheless, hiring the fourth person and creating a 4:1 staffing ratio would be considered the Best Cost Schedule, since it prevents employee burnout, fatigue, and operator error. If you are able to pay weekends at straight time, then adding the fourth person will save about $10,000 per year, per continuous position (assuming your labor rate is $10 per hour and benefit loading is between 35 and 40 percent).

Skill Balance

A successful sports team needs the right player at the right place at the right time. So does a successful 24-hour business. Since many 24-hour businesses require roughly the same type of work each hour, the scheduling system should provide skill balance around the clock to ensure better responsiveness and quality, fewer operational errors, and less downtime.

Ironically, in many 24-hour operations the most highly skilled individuals work the day shift and the less skilled are put on the back shifts (afternoons, nights, and weekends). It would be more logical to place the least skilled workers on the day shift, when managers, trainers, engineers, and other support staff are available, and the most highly skilled on the back shifts, when shift workers are more likely to face operating decisions on their own. In practice, this is rarely done. It's difficult enough to schedule equal skill balance across 24 hours.

Detecting the impact of skill imbalance is not always easy. Many manufacturing plants and continuous operations "just let it run" on the back shifts, and hence productivity is worse than on the day shift. At a European semiconductor plant, management was fooled into thinking it had decent skill balance because the evening and night shifts outproduced the day shift and the night shift output was equivalent to days. Actually, the night shift was 20 percent less productive than the day shift when disruptions from engineering and maintenance (which occur primarily during day shift) were subtracted out. Furthermore, with skill imbalance, the risk for costly operating or quality problems, which may go undetected until the next morning, is greater. Managers at a California silicon chip manufacturer found a $2 million error in the morning; an inexperienced night shift worker had destroyed a tray of silicon-processed wafers with the circuitry already etched. The plant manager told us that the employee "really felt bad about that."

Companies routinely have skill imbalance for two major reasons: (1) fixed shifts and (2) job bidding practices that reward seniority over qualification or allow migration from shift work to day work. From a strictly business needs perspective, rotating shifts avoid skill imbalance in 24-hour operations and may be advantageous and less costly.

Skill imbalance can be compounded in schedules that have both fixed shifts and fixed days off. At a nearly 100-year-old refinery in the eastern United States, the senior employees not only had the good shifts (days) but also all the weekends off, leaving the junior employees working weekends on the back shifts. Was it just a coincidence this refinery had a major fire on a Sunday afternoon, when the most senior person on that billion-dollar site that day had only five years of operating experience? Chapter 5 sets out a variety of options for fixing skill imbalance, including improving fixed shifts.

Covering Vacancies and Using Relief Personnel

Companies that are committed to 24-hour operations must be prepared to cover vacations, sickness, funeral leave, and other inevitable absences. The proper use of relief personnel is critical to the success of a 24-hour business; millions of dollars are at stake. Following are the most common methods for covering vacancies in a 24-hour business:

1. Shut down part of the operation.
2. Run short.
3. Cover with overtime.
    a. Call in on days off
    b. Split with 12s (Stay late, arrive early)
    c. Work doubles (16 hours; two 8-hour shifts)
    d. Quick comebacks (On 8 hours, off 8 hours, on 8 hours . . .)
4. Build in relief coverage on each crew.
5. Have a separate relief crew or relief operators.
6. Transfer a utility crew from discretionary workload to core workload.

Let's look at some of the methods. Each has merits and problems, and your solution will need to be tailored to your situation. Nevertheless, a few guidelines are worth considering. Shutting down operations or running short raises the question of whether your master schedule has too much overstaffing and idle time. Why not run short or shut down on a regular basis as part of your schedule, as opposed to waiting for an employee's suddenly being sick?

Covering with overtime can become expensive and cause considerable fatigue if it is overused. At an aluminum rolling mill in New York State, shift workers averaged 2,600 to 2,700 hours per year. Every single vacancy was covered—with overtime. Proper use of relief operators could have saved $1,152,000 per year routinely. Covering with overtime can be hard on employees too, if you call them in on their scheduled day off. It is also hard if you "split with 12s"—that is, ask them to split the uncovered shift so that they are now working a 12-hour shift. Worse yet is asking them to "work doubles"—to work two 8-hour shifts in a row, followed by a quick comeback, with only an 8-hour break between shifts. All of these "solutions," if carried out routinely, are unhealthy at the very least and could present a safety hazard.

Building relief staffing right into each shift crew (shift workers usually are unaware of this and there is no designated relief operator) is widely used in the older continuous-shift-work businesses. This can be an expensive system because of idle time; the extra staff will show up on back shifts when no one is absent. At one oil company with multiple U.S. refineries, idle time, which was due to relief staffing, was equivalent to 220,000 man-hours per year or $5,740,000 per year even after vacation and sick coverage was accounted for.

Be careful that your policy for covering vacancies does not inadvertently set up a costly incentive plan. In some shift work operations a sick worker is either being paid for the missed day or at the very least receiving a day off without pay, while another employee held over for coverage receives overtime pay. Using the "what goes around comes around" principle, the two employees may switch roles in the following week or month.

The most cost-effective approaches are having a separate relief crew on or bringing up a utility crew from the discretionary workload to cover the core workload. Goodyear Tire & Rubber in Lawton, Oklahoma, has built general operators into the staffing schedule to take over when other employees are on break in order to maximize capital utilization and core workload coverage. If you already have these internal relief operators, check to ensure they are scheduled efficiently.

Scheduling breaks, lunches, and relief in a Monday through Friday day shift operation may have only a small impact on your bottom line. But if you are operating around the clock and trying to maximize resources, the dollars can add up. A Japanese television manufacturer with 1,000 employees found that a modification in lunch policy kept the lines at full production with minimal relief requirements, with a savings of $850,000 a year. At a cigarette manufacturer in Australia with 275 operators, changing the schedule of only the relief operators by implementing 4-hour, part-time shifts gave a savings opportunity of $487,000 per year. Remember to separate the individual shift workers' schedule (they may each get 1 or 2 hours of breaks each day) from the operating schedule, which may run continuously for 24 hours.

Supervision

Three basic approaches are used for supervising coverage in 24-hour businesses (plus numerous variations). The traditional approach, most commonly found in the historic, continuous-process industries, is to have the same supervisor work with the same crew of shift workers year after year. This system achieves a good crew identity but has built-in weaknesses. Supervisors on a back shift, working with the same people on the same nonconventional day-off pattern, tend to overidentify with their crew until the supervisors lose their management identity. In addition, a feeling of being "stuck" with the same working crew may develop, so there is less emphasis on developing and improving skills and more acceptance of weaknesses and personnel problems.

A second approach, becoming quite common among American manufacturers, is self-directed shift work teams. There are no managers on the crews, and any crew member may become a team leader, a rotating assignment without extra pay. Each shift worker would then have the experience of being a leader and a follower, allowing a better perspective on managing a 24-hour business. Ideally, the prospective team leader would be trained and qualified in both operational and human resources skills.

The third approach is between these two alternatives: supervisors move from crew to crew every quarter or every year. The supervisors become a team whose mission is to work together and develop all of the employees they manage. Another advantage is that each hourly employee is evaluated by more than one person and has the opportunity to learn different ideas from different supervisors.

In some settings, especially where there are labor/management conflicts, getting supervisors and the hourly workers on the same schedule is impossible, a situation that could result in chaos—or be beneficial. Caltex Refinery, in Capetown, South Africa, had two groups of employees who could not agree on schedules: the supervisors, who wanted to keep their 8-hour schedule, and the unionized hourly work force, who wanted a new 12-hour shift. There was no room for compromise, and a strike was looming. The solution was to implement two totally different schedules for each group that nevertheless maintained communication between the supervisors and their hourly employees. Each hourly employee works with his or her primary supervisor on 80 percent of the workdays, and each supervisor sees his or her crew 65 percent of the workday. A simpler example of corresponding schedules is often used in mining industries, where supervisors' shift times are slightly staggered from the hourly. This system allows the supervisor to get a "heads up" (advance notice) so they can communicate to their crew prior to shift start.

Support Staff

Companies unfamiliar with running 24 hours a day are concerned that everyone will need to work around the clock, causing a tremendous increase in labor costs. This is not the case. As a general rule, at least one manager needs to be responsible for the entire business during off-hours. In case of any environmental problem, serious accident, personnel issue, or some other emergency, there should be a manager present with the necessary training and skills. Otherwise, there is no blanket rule on which other departments should also cover 24 hours. The greater the cross training (being skilled in 2 or more jobs or positions) and self-reliance of the shift work crew on duty, the less is the need for support staff to work around the clock. Traditional plants with strict job classifications and work limitations, on the other hand, need more around-the-clock support.

The major support group that needs to be evaluated and analyzed in a 24-hour business is usually maintenance. Some organizations have complete maintenance staffs that operate around the clock with their crews, a concept that promotes a team approach but can create overstaffing. The optimum method for scheduling is to develop a cross-trained operation-maintenance technician. If this is not possible, the bulk of the maintenance workers can be scheduled for a day shift schedule, with a minimum crew scheduled for off shifts and weekends. Preventive maintenance work should be part of the day time schedule, particularly if Best Equipment STrategy has been implemented; overtime should be used to cover unexpected, major equipment breakdown if maintenance people are not available.

Teams and Crews

A crew is a group of employees working the same hours with the same day-off pattern; a team is a group of employees working together for a common goal. Most shift work operations have a crew concept; fewer have a team concept. In our interviews of shift workers at client sites over the years, we have asked, "Do you really feel part of your crew?" and 84 percent answer "yes." But when we ask, "Do you really feel part of this company?" the response is only 59 percent "yes."

Management at a food manufacturer in Iowa thought it had a team concept when it really had a crew concept. The employees worked a 12-hour rotating shift system; two crews always saw each other but never the other two crews. When Crew A came in from their 4 days off, they spent the first 90 minutes of their 12-hour shift resetting all of the controls to make sure the process ran "their way." Subsequently the other crews made their own adjustment, resulting in four different operating strategies.

Each crew handled maintenance differently as well. Crews B and C learned new maintenance skills required for their equipment and were able to respond to most routine breakdowns. But Crews A and D still relied on the daytime support team, often incurring significant downtime on their night shifts. The managers at this site believed they had an advanced team system because they let the crews handle responsibilities such as hiring and covering vacancies. However, the crew concept was so ingrained that when one team member returned from a six-month assignment from Desert Storm, he insisted on being put back into his crew (he was) despite the fact he had been replaced and was needed on another crew.

Like most other shift workers, the primary allegiance was to the crew, not the total operation. Because the employees were happy with their day-off pattern, we added a multipurpose crew (MPC), which is a schedule system whereby each operator has a "home crew" but also spends part of each year working with a smaller crew made up of employees from each of the other home crews. (It's sort of like basketball's all-star Dream Team, with members of different teams coming together once in a while to form a new team.) This system allowed time for members of the four crews to share ideas, work together, and slowly evolve into one team. By converting idle time to production time, the plant did not have to hire additional employees to build the MPC and in fact reduced labor costs by $400,000 per year.

Scheduling Teams

Many companies use self-directed work teams to lower costs and improve processes. If you have similar technology to your competition but fewer layers of management, faster decision time, more customer-supplier contact, and better use of available knowledge, you may be able to build a cost advantage of 10 to 30 percent. To achieve these cost savings requires a major change in how shift workers are perceived. A few decades ago, the supervisor was the brain of a 24-hour facility, and the shift workers provided the muscle. Today, more and more shift workers are knowledge workers or technology workers, and may even have direct customer interaction. At Mead Publishing's paper division in Escanaba, Michigan, the schedule when the plant first opened in 1967 was 6-hour shifts, 365 days per year, and no days off because the shift work jobs were completely physical. Today, schedules with built-in training are being developed. Shift schedules can be designed to strengthen teamwork or to prevent it.

Advanced schedules build in time for discretionary workload while the core workload is being covered. Schedules that originated in the 1930s, or even the 1970s, are unlikely to build in time for discretionary workloads. As a result, all of these desired value-added activities may become schedule busters—events that don't fit into the master schedule and cause overtime, stress, poor employee morale, or equipment downtime, or simply are not done due to the pressures to maintain production. You'll know your facility is in this mode when you hear shift workers complain, "I have to come in on my time off to solve their [management's] problem."

Advanced shift schedules and teamwork go hand in hand. An agriculture chemical plant in Alberta, Canada, uses a utility crew made up of shift workers to talk to customers about their products. On one occasion they learned that the fertilizer they were producing was ineffective during heavy rain. They went back to the plant and worked on the product until it was improved to their clients' satisfaction. At Scott Paper Company's new mill in Owensboro, Kentucky, shift workers handle every function, from ordering new products, to production, to calling customers and arranging shipments, to personnel, payroll, and administration. Their work schedule includes a rotation through core work and discretionary work. At Ultramar Refining in Los Angeles, shift workers on the MPC establish common operating procedures and a standardized training program. Tom Weber, operations manager at Ultramar, reports, "The people who are on it love it [they temporarily work day shift with 3-day weekends]. They've died and gone to heaven and are even getting into writing procedures."

Many of our clients have found that if the first team activity is fixing the shift work schedules, a win-win, employees will more willingly accept the team concept.

Here are examples of activities that are built into shift work schedules:

- Training
- Productivity improvements
- Process flow improvement
- Customer delivery improvement
- Visits to customers
- Visits to suppliers
- Statistical process control
- Team meetings
- Community service
- Work redesign
- Hiring
- Personnel
- Administration
- Establish common operating and safety procedures
- Benchmarking against competitors and pacesetters
- Shift work schedule improvement

Dedicated Training Time

Training is essential to improving quality, productivity, flexibility, speed, and competitiveness. Most businesses recognize this fact and budget significant money for training, sometimes a few percentage points of the entire labor budget. But because most 24-hour businesses do not have a systematic training schedule built into their shift work schedules in an organized manner, training becomes a schedule buster, causing production to suffer or increasing overtime. Among the conflicting demands of production, meeting customer needs, limiting overtime, and training, training usually gets the axe. Training efficiency and the speed and level of accomplished training falls behind. If companies truly recognized the importance of training and its impact on the business, training would become an integral part of the schedule and not be so easily pushed aside. In nuclear power plants, where shift workers train about 350 hours per year, training is mandated by law, including classroom training and simulation. Shift schedules can be designed to build in any amount of training, in any sequence required—for example, 40 hours every 6 weeks (Pennsylvania Power & Light), 1.25 hours a week (Toshiba), 90 hours per year (Chevron).

Communication for the 24-Hour Workforce

Maintaining good communication with a day workforce is challenging enough; in a 24-hour business, your carefully constructed messages may not even reach the back shifts. Shift workers also complain that they're out of touch; only 32 percent of the thousands of shift workers we interview every year report that "management pays the same attention to shift workers as they do to day workers." Fifty-six percent of these same shift workers report that their primary source of information about their job and company comes through the grapevine, 28 percent from team meetings, 11 percent from their immediate supervisor, and only 5 percent from higher management. Even at one high-tech communication manufacturer, 83 percent of the *shift supervisors* reported they got their information from the grapevine. Poor communication leads to poor morale, overlooked steps, unnecessary repetition, and wasted efforts. Good communication enables lessons learned to be passed on to succeeding shifts as opposed to repeating and/or compounding mistakes.

Not only are communications difficult from shift to shift and crew to crew but also between different departments, especially when administration, engineering, maintenance, laboratory, payroll, and human resources have a day shift schedule while production is on shift work. If subsequent shifts are not fully informed as to the status of their project, steps may be eliminated or duplicated. We worked at one gold mine where it was not unusual for a truck to have its spark plugs changed twice during a 12-hour period. The second shift, not sure of what the first had done, unnecessarily repeated this process.

Although communication will never be perfect in a 24-hour

operation, it is just as easy to design schedules that facilitate employee communication as it is to design schedules that complicate it. At a Sandoz Chemical plant in South Carolina that manufactures hundreds of different dyes, a schedule with a 7-day break resulted in significant production and customer errors. A new schedule has each crew meeting with the current production crew when they report in after their two new 4- or 5-day breaks. The results are better communication and fewer customer order errors.

Poor communication is often accepted as part of the culture. Dynamic process changes do not filter down to every worker if half the work force is on a Sunday through Wednesday schedule while the other half works Wednesday through Saturday. The Sunday through Wednesday group starts its workweek with no direct communication with management. Crews coming in to relieve each other may start to make decisions on what products to turn out based on what they believe is required as opposed to finding out what is required.

There are solutions to these problems. At Motorola in Austin, Texas, some human resources managers are scheduled for shift work. Similar scheduling solutions would work for a plant manager. If employees are truly your greatest asset, should not the site manager see or talk with every shift worker at least once a week, even if only for 10 to 15 minutes? This can be easily accomplished if the plant manager has a flexible schedule that allows late hours to be rewarded with time off (otherwise, burnout will make it impossible to maintain a day worker and shift worker status for long). Use the grapevine to advantage. A manager talking to just a few shift workers on the back shift is guaranteed to get his or her message sent everywhere!

Other methods to maintain good shift communications in a 24-hour business include voicemail, electronic mail, log books, shift handovers, crew-to-crew turnover meetings, "hot changes" (changing at the work station but not stopping the equipment), and staggered start times for hourly workers and/or supervisors (allowing gradual shift changes). Still, there's nothing like regular face-to-face informal meetings. Involve your shift workers in determining what type, frequency, and length of communication everyone needs.

Avoid scheduling communication meetings at the end of a

shift, especially at the end of the night shift. Employees are tired and focused on going home so that retention may be nearly zero. If your schedule is designed properly you should be able to meet with one crew while still providing coverage with another crew. Of course, occasionally the entire communication-coverage system is broken. After an all-day consultation with the state police in an eastern U.S. state, I needed directions to get to the airport as quickly as possible. The police told me it was okay to drive fast between 3:00 and 3:30 P.M. because there are no state police on the road at that time. It's shift change; everyone was at roll call or going home, and no one was on duty!

One Manager's Perspective

Tom Meyers is the operation manager for one of Portland General Electric's power plants in Boardman, Oregon, a company that has been running shift work since 1899. He has a good deal of experience with communication, crew, team, and discretionary workload issues:

> One of the major problems with shift work is that when you are trying to operate with approximately four to six crews, depending on what kind of shift schedule you have, you actually have four to six different individual groups that are operating a plant with very little interaction. They become semiautonomous and independent, and they feel they know the best way to operate. From a business point of view, it's very hard to have consistent rules, operating practices, and safety practices when each individual crew seems to feel that it is a small company unto itself and operates that way.
>
> On our new schedule, without adding new personnel, we've increased to a six-crew rotation, plus we've added a multipurpose crew. This has given us the one thing that we were never able to complete previously: time for special projects and particularly training, which was our company's concern with the previous schedule. The schedule is definitely better in that it provides a

more consistent operation. I'm able to plan and conduct training that we were not able to do before.

Conclusion

We have spent this chapter looking at shift work from the business viewpoint and found that schedules based on your business needs can convert costs into profits, but if you focus *only* on business needs, and then make a schedule change, you will probably fail! Schedules that do not meet health and safety standards can result in catastrophic accidents and environmental damage and cost millions of dollars, and if the shift workers don't like their work schedules, they will make your business unproductive. Shift workers have the ultimate veto power. Let's take a look in the next chapters how health and safety and employee desires are critical in finding the Best Cost Schedule.

3

Health and Safety Requirements

The night shift workers at a southwestern manufacturing plant had no supper during one shift. The reason was that a sleepy forklift truck driver had crashed into the lunchroom, impaled the refrigerator, and destroyed the meals.

Though this story is retold with humor, it is not funny. Only a decade ago, driving home intoxicated after a party was considered a sign of machismo; today there is greater awareness, outrage, and demand for restitution for accidents related to drunken driving. Similarly, sleepy workers are starting to be a serious concern instead of a laughing matter, as communities become aware of life-threatening accidents and catastrophes related to shift work. The worst industrial accidents in recent years have occurred in shift work operations. Three Mile Island, Chernobyl, Bhopal, and *Exxon Valdez* are frequently cited examples. More recently, sleepiness at work has attracted the attention of the legal profession. In New York, the parents of a woman who died after being rushed to the hospital with a high fever sued, charging sleep-deprived doctors killed her by giving her the wrong medication. Shift schedules are also coming under legal scrutiny. A McDonalds restaurant in Portland, Oregon, was found negligent after a part-time student-worker had a fatal accident on the way home from an extra over-time shift (3:30 P.M.–8:00 A.M.) offered by his supervisor.

Who is responsible for the actions of a sleepy employee? The company? The employee? Or some other party? Who will decide what the regulations will be? Only a few industries, such as the transportation field, have federal guidelines for hours of work and rest, but most of the policies originated in the 1930s, well before modern sleep research began, and they are outdated. Moreover, enforcement of regulations is sporadic. There is often a large discrepancy between the master schedule, which may be safe, and the actual schedules that are worked. While these legal issues are being worked out, approximately 20 million Americans will work shift work this week, including several million who must be awake all night while most of us are sleeping.

Some Telling Statistics

Our shift worker database shows that 59 percent report falling asleep at work on a regular basis during night shift, 28 percent on day shift, and 22 percent on afternoon shift. These results do not include episodes of falling asleep during lunch or breaks, only while actually working. The numbers are pretty consistent year to year, country to country, and industry to industry. They do vary by shift schedule, however. Predictably, schedules that are more difficult for the human body to cope with result in more sleepiness.

We also ask shift workers if they have seen poor safety practices or experienced poor performance due to sleepiness: 68 percent have seen poor performance or operational errors due to sleepiness, and 53 percent have seen poor safety practice or accidents due to fatigue. Quality can suffer due to sleepiness as well. It's not unusual for conscientious shift workers to pack poor-quality product at 3:00 A.M. but remain too fatigued and unmotivated to care—a direct result of fatigue. Figure 3-1 lists some of the impact of sleepiness shift workers have reported to us on confidential questionnaires when we asked them to describe errors, near misses, or poor performance they observed at their plants as a result of sleepiness on jobs where they were likely to "nod off."

With improved automation, fewer shift work employees are responsible for more powerful technologies. In any of the nation's nuclear power plants, roughly fifteen shift workers are responsible for plant operations during the night shift. Only two shift workers operate the newest and most modern electric utility in Australia at night. What happens if they fall asleep on the job?

Remember, these employees are not sleeping on the floor or

Figure 3-1. Errors, near misses, and poor performance observed on the part of shift workers due to sleepiness and jobs where they are likely to "nod off."

"On grave, not having the drive to provide a thorough job. In an electric cart, I hit a water hydrant protector and was bruised badly. I did not report incident."

"Letting equipment sit idle waiting on operator, wrong data entry, missing data, slow work pace, doing things over again because not done correctly."

"Co-worker almost burned himself on furnace due to not being alert."

"Taking extra break times because of sleeping and not returning on time."

"Wrapping machine jams. Slitter jams. Machines running without monitoring."

"Walking into walls. Driving forklifts into inanimate objects. Forgetting things."

"Operators drop things on line. Pens, sticks, scrapers. Then they go through the machinery."

"Hands getting caught in machine (wrapping)."

"I fall asleep when I stay over on the cutter, every time."

"Missing defective product as it goes by."

"Sending out product without a code. Untaped boxes."

"High scrap rates off machines due to people not being alert."

"Once in a while I I feel that I just don't notice jams or other obvious problems as quickly as usual. I never nod off or sleep at work."

"With the audible alarms off (which they usually are), there are times when visual alarms are not noticed in a timely fashion."

"Belts overloading, bins filling, and people not seeing."

"I saw a mechanic almost electrocuted because of lack of awareness due to sleepiness."

"I placed a plastic boat in a bake oven. Destroyed a 25-wafer lot. Also this caused contamination to the oven. Due to overwork on a 12-hour shift on the weekend."

"Falling off chairs, pouring wrong acid, misprocess, bad attitude."

"Wrong programs in etchers. When driving home start to nod off. Just don't feel like working."

"More errors as far as inputting data. Downloading wrong recipes when running equipment."

"Putting in wrong times for runs, putting the wrong material in the furnace."

"Misprogramming. Misaligned probe needles—can't focus eyes."

"Lams (metal discs) falling out of shoot, letting strip go up in die, letting oil run on floor."

"Working with 350-degree oil; if you're not careful the discs drop out at you and you get burned."

"Entering data at CRTs. On maker lines when they are running food and workload is slack."

"Control room operators tend to get sleepy on night shift between the hours of 3–5 A.M."

"Jobs that require monitoring instruments closely for extended periods."

on a cot while they are working but are likely to nod off right at their work station. There are occasional but more blatant examples of shift workers' bedding down, sleeping at work, and neglecting their duties. For example, in August 1988 the Nuclear Regulatory Commission closed a nuclear power plant for more than a year after operators were found actually sleeping on duty; this was not just a rare event of nodding off. The company was fined $1.25 million for failing to manage their shift workers, and thirty-three control room operators were fined $500 to $1,000 apiece. The plant is owned by several different utilities, and the managing partner was sued by its co-owners for over $250 million in costs resulting from the plant's shutdown.

In some industries, unofficial semisanctioned sleeping on the job is a standard practice. For example, in mines, a dragline, an enormous shovel five stories high costing over $50 million, really requires only one or two employees to operate it, but it may be staffed with two or three individuals so the employees can informally relieve each other when they get tired. Management knows it could cut back on manning, but the current system keeps the dragline running nearly continuously and safely. Officially sanctioned night shift napping reportedly is common in Japan and unofficially is common in many industries, such as nursing and medicine.

For the most part, the sleepy shift worker is a motivated employee who is struggling to ward off the uncontrollable, irresistible urge to sleep. Frequently shift workers experience microsleeps (very brief episodes of sleep mixed in with wakefulness). *Microsleep* is a phenomenon that almost every human has experienced when sleep deprived, during activities such as driving a car. It's possible to have your eyes open but your brain is asleep. These episodes usually last for a few seconds, though longer episodes, up to 20 minutes, have been documented with electrophysiological monitors. Typically the driver or shift worker can't believe he or she fell asleep.

If the statistics that show roughly half the shift work force nodding off during work on a regular basis are accurate, what is really amazing is the small number of industrial accidents that occur. Despite numerous media claims that sleepiness causes infamous accidents such as that at Three Mile Island, it's too simplistic to say Three Mile Island (TMI) happened at 4:00 A.M.; therefore shift work and sleepy workers are to blame. What about the billions of safe man-hours of operations in other nuclear plants, chemical plants, tankers, refineries, and airlines, and the thousands of large tankers that pass safely through narrow channels every week? Although the four control room operators at TMI on duty were completing their fifth consecutive night shift (11:00 P.M.–7:00 A.M.), sleepiness and shift work were not found to be a contributing factor in subsequent investigations. Poorly designed controls, inadequate training, and panic were the primary causes.* The operators overrode the automatic safety systems and turned a minor glitch into a potential disaster. Ironically, if the operators had been on break, eating lunch, or sleeping when the alarms and flashing lights went off at 4:00 A.M., there probably would have been only minor damage to Unit 2 and possibly no accident at all.

Exxon *Valdez:* An Expensive Shift Change

The Exxon *Valdez* catastrophe is a good example of how poor shift work scheduling can play a role in a disaster. Although alcohol is frequently cited as the primary cause of the accident, the captain, who had been drinking, was not on duty at the time of the accident, and the employee at the helm during the actual accident was not asleep at the wheel, but a shift change was taking place.

The Exxon *Valdez* accident occurred on March 24, 1989. Ten million gallons of oil spilled over 1,300 square miles—the largest U.S. environmental disaster ever. The captain of the vessel, Joseph Hazelwood, was asleep in his cabin shortly after midnight. Normally, second mate Lloyd LeCain would have been on duty, but because LeCain had just finished working a long shift, the inexperienced third mate, Gregory Cousins, decided to let LeCain continue sleeping. Cousins took control of the vessel and finally grounded atop a reef. Cousins had had between 3.5 and 6 hours of time off in the previous 12 hours and was working overtime at the time of

*Shift work operations can still learn a great deal from Three Mile Island: Human factors (man-machine interface), training, control room layout, decision making, teamwork, and operator reaction to emergencies can be improved.

the accident, but there was no evidence he fell asleep while turning the 211,000-ton vessel.

John Hillman and John Spence, officers of the Seaman's Union whose members worked on the Exxon *Valdez*, point to crew reduction problems. Because of crew reductions, both Spence and Hillman said, posts can go vacant for periods of up to 15 minutes during shift changes on a vessel the size of the Exxon *Valdez*. This vacancy occurs because of the time it takes to walk from one end of the ship to the other. It also occurs when the crew members are required to perform duties in addition to maintaining their assigned posts.

Both situations apparently occurred simultaneously as midnight approached on March 23: A shift change was in process just before the Exxon *Valdez* ran aground, and lookout Maureen Jones, carrying the pilot ladder, was assisting Cousins in letting off the harbor pilot instead of being on lookout.

Poor shift work scheduling, human error, excessive overtime, crew fatigue, inappropriate sleep schedules, inadequate shift changes, alcohol, insufficient cross training, and reduced crew sizes were the underlying causes of the accident.

The Two Key Factors

Operating more hours, across more time zones, with instantaneous communication, means more stress on one's *biological clock*—a biological system designed for living in one time zone, without electric light, matching the rising and setting of the sun in a simpler environment.

Some people say that the human body is meant to sleep during the night and be awake during the day, so there can never be a solution to the biological clock problem. But that's not necessarily true. We know that humans can transport themselves to time zones that are totally opposite their home, sleep, and wake times and make the adjustment.

For those of us who have to deal with shift work operators today and tonight, let's start by understanding the two key factors that will determine their alertness on the job. (The factors, which interact, are shown in Figure 3-2.) Factor I is your *circadian rhythm*: Is it in or out of sync? *Circadian* is a Latin word. *Circa* means "about," *dies* means "a day," or your daily rhythm. In simpler terms, if the clock on the wall at work says 8:00 A.M. and your brain clock is reading 8:00 A.M., you are in sync, and you can function well. However, if the clock on the wall says 8:00 A.M. and your brain clock is registering 3:00 A.M., you are going to be out of sync and struggling to be alert. If the clock at work says 3:00 A.M. and your biological clock is set for peak performance, you'll be alert and function fine.

But Factor I is only half the story. Factor II is your daily sleep requirement. You can be completely in sync and still be sleepy at work if you are not meeting your daily sleep requirement. Imagine you are a straight day worker needing 8 hours of sleep per day but getting only 2 to 3 hours. You have built up a significant sleep debt. Even though your circadian rhythm is in sync, lack of sleep may put you at risk for an accident.

In the best shift work scheduling systems, the employees are doing well on both Factor I and Factor II. In the worst scheduling systems (we call them "zombie schedules") employees are having severe problems with both their circadian rhythms and their sleep debt.

Factor I: Circadian Rhythms

Let's discuss Factor I in more detail. The body's circadian rhythms are regulated by a group of 10,000 brain cells (about the size of a pinhead) located in the hypothalamus. The specific location is called the suprachiasmatic nucleus (SCN). A special nerve pathway called the retinohypothalamic tract conveys information about light and darkness in the outside environment entering the eyes to the SCN.

The SCN, or biological clock, takes this information and orchestrates the timing of physiological cycles in the body. For example, the SCN controls when certain hormones are released into the bloodstream and when they are not. Over 100 functions, including metabolism, digestion, and the sleep-wake cycle (sleep and wake-up times) are under the control of this timing mechanism.

Figure 3-2. Circadian rhythms and total sleep time.

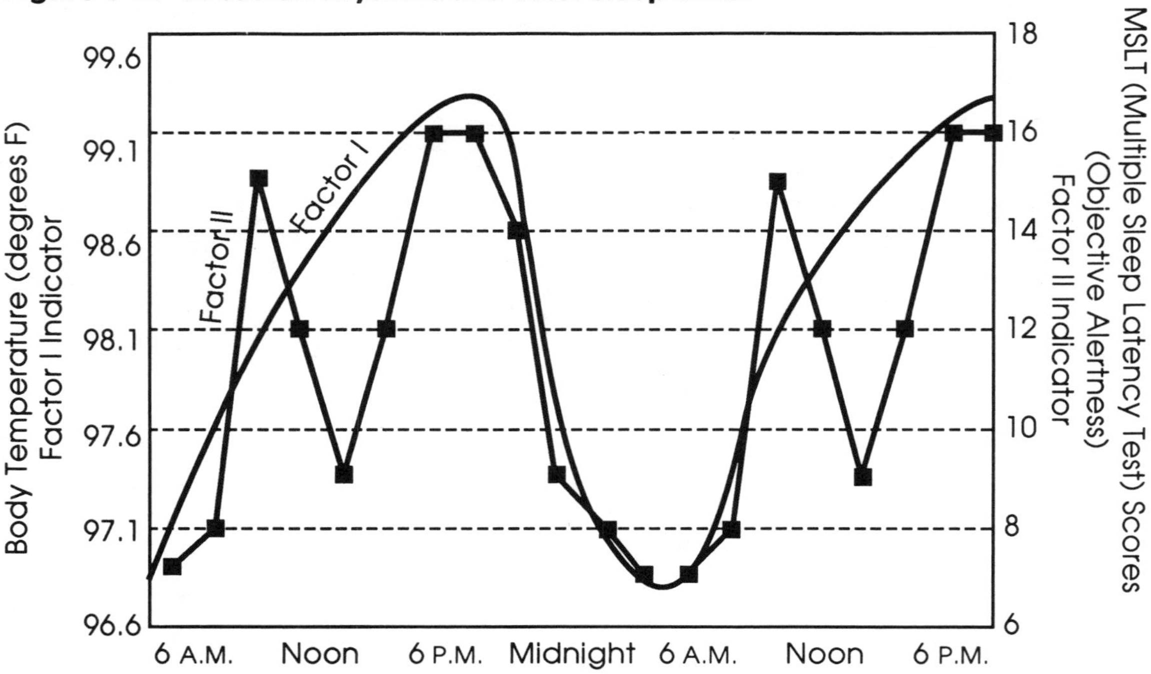
Body Temperature (degrees F)
Factor I Indicator
99.6
99.1
98.6
98.1
97.6
97.1
96.6
MSLT (Multiple Sleep Latency Test) Scores
(Objective Alertness)
Factor II Indicator
18
16
14
12
10
8
6
Factor I
Factor II
6 A.M.
Noon
6 P.M.
Midnight
6 A.M.
Noon
6 P.M.

Factor I: Circadian rhythm fluctuates every 24 hours.
Factor II: Sleep debt results in an afternoon dip for most adults.

Scientists have learned from experimental animal research and patients with small tumors that without the SCN, humans become cat nappers without sustained periods of sleep and wakefulness, sleeping several more hours per day than is typical. If we did not have a biological clock to wake us up, we might sleep about 12 hours a day, but we would sleep at random times. There could never be a Super Bowl. Half of the audience would be asleep, half of the team would be asleep, and half of the other players might be just waking up, because everyone would be out of sync. One of the functions of the biological clock is to organize a species, or society.

The biological clock developed when human activity was largely confined to daytime hours and most humans lived not only within one time zone but within a few miles' radius. In this simple world, in anticipation of waking up each morning the body clock would help mobilize energy and metabolism, jump-starting each person for the day. In just the past 100 years, a mere instant in the human time scale, we have entered a new time dimension with jet travel, invention of the lightbulb, and our 24-hour society.

Unlike the pacemaker in your heart, which you can touch and feel, indicating it's beating about once a second, this SCN pacemaker is harder to measure. You can't feel it, you can't see it, and it beats or cycles only about once every 24 hours. Nevertheless, it has a big impact on your body, especially if you are on shift work. Even willpower can not overcome this tiny biological clock.

One way to find out what time it is in your body is to measure your temperature for 24 hours. As Figure 3-2 indicates, the body temperature is not constant at 98.6 degrees F but fluctuates by 2 to 3 degrees a day, its 24-hour rhythm controlled by the SCN pacemaker. When your internal-core body temperature is high or rising, you may be more alert. When the body temperature is at its nadir, you should be sound asleep in bed. Ideally, the best time to work is when your temperature, and your alertness, are at their peak. When the body temperature is at its low point is the best time to be in the middle of your sleep period. For a shift worker coming to his or her first night shift, 3:00 to 4:00 A.M. will usually be the lowest point of the biological day and the hours associated with extreme drowsiness and urge to sleep. A few hours later (when the shift ends at 8:00 A.M.), they may struggle to fall asleep at home because the internal alarm clock believes it's time to prime the body to wake up.

Those of you who have never worked shift work have still probably experienced this phenomenon. If you recall an all-night party, you probably got up on Friday at 7:00 A.M., went to school, then stayed up all night, not going to sleep until Saturday morning at 7:00 A.M. Because you had been up 24 hours, you probably thought you would sleep your normal 8 hours and perhaps make up about 3 or 4 extra hours of sleep. But in fact, most individuals who go to sleep after an all-night party or all-night plane ride find that when they try to fall asleep at around 8:00 A.M. they'll get 4 or 5 hours of poor-quality sleep. The reason is that they are trying to sleep when their body clock is set to wake up.

The body clock affects shift rotations. Clockwise rotations require a shift change to later hours. For example, after working 7 A.M. to 3 P.M. for a week, you go to the 3 P.M. to 11 P.M. shift for a week. Counterclockwise rotation would be going from a week on the 7 A.M. to 3 P.M. shift to a week on the 11 P.M. to 7 A.M. shift. It is more difficult for the human biological clock and is associated with greater health problems.

In 1986, I discussed extensively how the body clock can adjust.* The most common shift schedule at that time was a weekly counterclockwise rotating schedule (employees went from days to nights to evenings to days), which essentially forced shift workers to travel around the world in 4 weeks, always going in an eastbound direction. Since that schedule has become rare, almost extinct, I will not repeat that information in this book but will review a few key points.

If we could make the biological clock adjust 100 percent, then most of the health, safety, and performance problems specific to night work could be avoided, assuming the employees were also getting 8 or 9 hours of sleep. For example, for many day workers, 10:00 A.M. is a peak time of day for feeling alert. If you could feel like that during an entire night shift, there would be no significant, inherent risk in working nights. So the question is, Can you adjust your body rhythms? The answer is yes, but it is extremely difficult without the proper environment. How do we know that we can

*Wide Awake at 3 A.M. (New York: W. H. Freeman, 1986).

adjust the rhythms? We know that individuals who travel from New York to Perth, Australia, a 180-degree shift, adapt their sleep and wake times without a problem within a week.

In order for employees to adapt completely to night shift, however, they would have to work enough consecutive nights so that their rhythms would invert 180 degrees. They would also have to manage their outside life so that it was geared toward sleeping during the day and being alert at night. Lighting would need to be manipulated in their environment to support the transition, ideally equivalent to sunlight during the night shift and blackness during the day hours when they are sleeping. This idealized approach would also require extremely understanding family and friends. But even without these dramatic measures, the biological clock can be adjusted slightly about 2 or 3 hours a day, like adjusting after a jet flight from New York to Denver.

Using Bright Lights to Reset the Circadian Clock

Manipulation of light-dark cycles has long been an established method of influencing biological growth cycles in plants and activity patterns in animals. Exposure to bright light can reset the biological clock in humans as well, depending on the timing and intensity of the exposure. Exposure to bright light toward the end of the usual sleep period (for example, 4 A.M.) is interpreted by the biological clock as a dawn signal (a new day is starting) and can advance the clock, initiating a period of activity. Exposure to bright enough light near the end of the normal active period (awake hours) will delay the clock (prolonged dusk), causing a delay shift. (Normal indoor light is 150 lux; a bright office is 500 lux; sunlight exposure ranges from 10,000 lux on a cloudy day to 100,000 lux on a sunny day at the beach. Exposure for night shift workers is targeted in the 5,000–10,000 lux range.)

Research carried out by Dr. Charles Czeisler at Harvard University has shown that strategically scheduled exposure to bright light enables shift workers to manipulate their biological rhythms. An initial pilot project at San Diego Gas & Electric indicates that exposure to a flexible intensity of bright light, equivalent to low-level sunlight, and 8 hours of sleep in total darkness during the daytime, results in a 180-degree-phase shift of the body clock within 24 hours, with resulting improved alertness and better sleep. Manipulating light in this way could give shift workers the advantage that jet travelers have. These factory workers are like travelers to a new time zone, where all of the cues help adjustment. In the future, a combination of bright lights and proper scheduling and possibly hormone-pharmaceutical manipulation (chronobiotics) may solve the Factor I problem for shift workers.

Factor II: Daily Sleep Requirement

Adjusting for Factor I, circadian rhythms, is only half the battle. The other key element is Factor II, your daily sleep requirement, or how large your sleep debt is. You can be totally in sync, but if you are chronically sleep deprived, it's not going to matter very much that you are in sync.

How much sleep do you need? In the 1970s, hundreds of thousands of dollars of U.S. government grant money was spent on answering this question. After years of research at many different locations, the conclusion was that you need enough sleep to be alert the next day. (As my colleagues in Australia would say, "Brilliant, mate!") This was not a sufficient answer, but the underlying concept made sense. A person who had enough sleep the previous night should be completely alert—so alert that he or she should be unable to nod off or take a nap.

Alertness and its opposite, sleepiness, is a physiological state that can be accurately measured. If you have no sleep debt at all (which means you had enough sleep the previous night), then even finding yourself in a hot room, after a heavy meal, reading an economics textbook, you would not be able to nod off.

Researchers at the Stanford Sleep Clinic developed the Multiple Sleep Latency Test to measure alertness throughout the day. (MSLT scores are shown in Figure 3-3 as an indicator of daily sleep requirement.) It's a simple test. An individual (volunteer, patient, shift worker, etc.) is brought into a dark, quiet room at 10:00 A.M. Just before entering the room, a few electrodes are attached to the scalp to measure brain activity and the person is hooked up to a polygraph, so clinicians can definitively determine whether he or she is awake or asleep. At 10:00 A.M., the lights are turned off, and

Figure 3-3. MSLT profile for three groups with different amounts of nocturnal sleep.

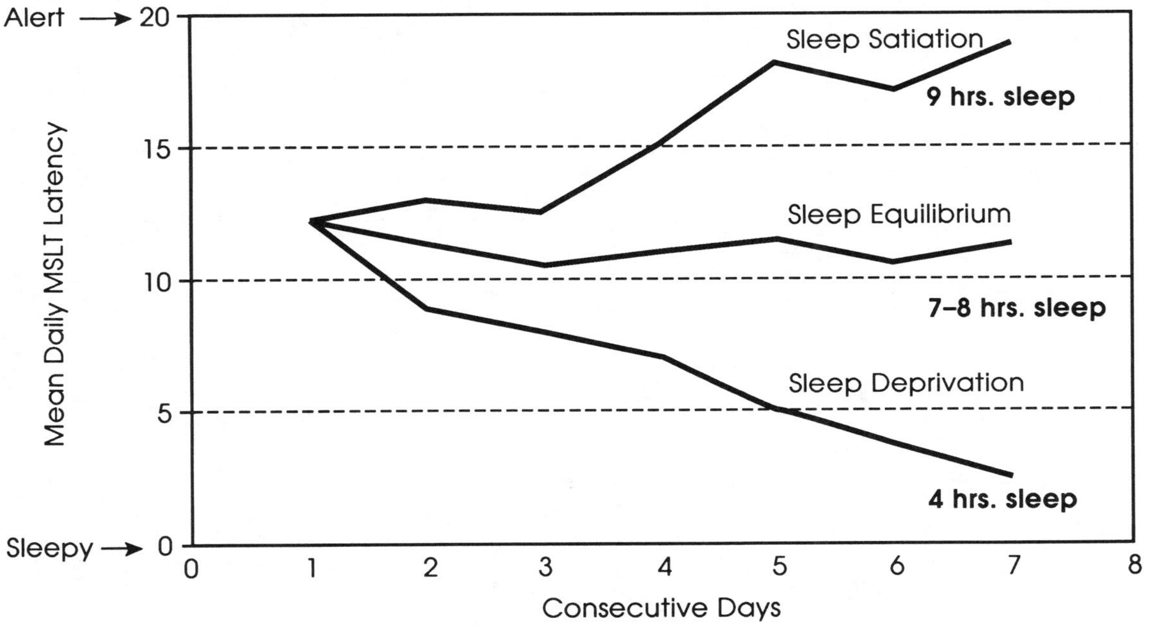

the individual is given an opportunity to sleep. A person who falls asleep in 4 minutes gets a score of 4—a sleep latency of 4 minutes; if he or she falls asleep in 15 minutes, the score is 15. If after 20 minutes the person is still awake, the test is ended, and the person gets a score of 20, indicating peak alertness. Their first sleep latency test is over.

The sleep latency test is repeated again at noon, 2:00 P.M., 4:00 P.M., and 6:00 P.M.—every 2 hours throughout the day. Then an MSLT profile, or average daily score, is calculated. Figure 3-3 indicates the MSLT results of three groups of day shift volunteers. One group (sleep satiation) was allowed 9 hours of sleep every night for a week, the second group (sleep equilibrium) 7–8 hours sleep per night and the third group (sleep deprivation) only 4 hours. After 1 week, the sleep satiation group members improved their MSLT scores each day until they were so alert that they were essentially unable to fall asleep in the nap test. The sleep equilibrium group remained constant, with the ability to fall asleep on daytime nap tests within 12 minutes. The sleep deprivation group showed a successive drop in daytime alertness; by the end of the week they could nod off in the nap test within 3 minutes, equivalent to a diagnosis of narcolepsy, a serious genetic disorder of excessive sleepiness.

Outside the lab, the most alert Americans are 10-year-old children. This age group sleeps 9 to 10 hours per day, maintains a consistent bedtime and wake time 7 days a week, does not use caffeine, sleeping pills, or alcohol, and does not follow unusual work schedules. Perhaps it's not surprising that most adults who do not follow these practices can fall asleep in 10 to 15 minutes when given a chance to nod off.

Most adults blame their sleepiness on the environment—the boring meeting, the lights off, the monotony of the job, or the long drive. But they're wrong. Someone who is physiologically alert—that is, had enough sleep the previous night—cannot nod off (even in a boring meeting). But if someone is sleep deprived, and most adults are, then the environment will play a key role. For example, an individual who has had little sleep and is about to fall asleep in the control room may be able to overcome sleepiness if the plant manager strolls in unexpectedly. The human species is adaptable.

We can overcome our sleep debt on a short-term basis, but the best plan is to avoid sleep debt in the first place.

As a group most shift workers on the MSLT, depending on the schedule, fall slightly below the sleep satiation group with a score average of about 8. In a study done at Stanford, one group of shift workers who napped prior to their night shift always maintained an MSLT profile greater than 12, whereas another group that did not nap had their MSLT score reduced close to 4 minutes during the 3:30 A.M. and 6:30 A.M. tests.

On the basis of these data, we conclude that the average adult needs 9 hours of sleep per 24 hours in order to be fully alert during waking hours.* In today's fast-paced world, everyone is trying to do more in less time. Something has to give, and what normally gives is sleep. Most of us have a deficit in our sleep bank.

Sleep Debt

Although not as famous as the budget deficit, the sleep deficit is now getting national attention, including on the covers of *Time* and *Newsweek* and the front page of *The Wall Street Journal*.

Here are some signs of sleep debt:

- You experience powerful waves of drowsiness at meetings, lectures, or classes, especially if this occurs at times other than around 2:00 P.M.
- You rely on the alarm clock to wake you.
- You struggle to get awake and get going after you wake up.
- You doze off without wanting to.
- You doze off easily while reading or watching TV.
- You feel sleepy after a single glass of beer or wine.
- You have little energy after dinner.
- You don't feel alert and energetic.

Most people no longer know what it feels like to be fully alert. The average day worker is getting about 7.5 hours of sleep, so he or she is building up a consistent, moderate sleep debt. The prob-

*There are individual differences; some people require fewer hours and some more to maintain peak alertness; however, most individuals who sleep less than 9 hours will have documented sleepiness on the MSLT.

lem for shift workers is even greater. The average worker on night shift obtains 5.82 hours of sleep (including naps) per 24 hours; on the day shift and afternoon shift, it's not much better: 6.53 hours and 6.76 hours, respectively. Many shift workers try to "make up" sleep on their long weekend breaks, averaging 7.58 hours of sleep on those days, but it's too late. If you were already sleep deprived in the previous days, your performance suffered. You didn't feel well then and when you "catch up," you probably feel groggy on the first day you get extra recovery sleep. Therefore, sleep debt interferes with time off as well.

Although most people function with a chronic mild sleep debt, shift workers have a much greater debt, since it accumulates. A shift worker on seven consecutive shifts, conservatively needing 8 hours of sleep per day but getting only 6, has built up a debt of 14 hours. That has the same impact on his or her functioning as missing 1 to 2 nights of sleep. Manufacturing workers scheduled for one weekend of overtime end up working 12 consecutive days. Most employees working through the weekends are going to try to fit in day-off activities after work shifts. Time is borrowed from the sleep bank, and the likelihood of getting even 6 hours of sleep diminishes.

Developing shift schedules based solely on Factor II would suggest that shift schedules should provide frequent days off to recuperate. Working one, two, or three shifts in a row, followed by several days off to recuperate, will help return sleep debt to zero.

Preventing Sleep Debt

How can you overcome sleep debt? The best way is to prevent it in the first place. Obtaining the right amount of sleep each day is the safest plan because the ability to predict when you might nod off during a task is limited. In one study at Stanford using accurate physiological monitoring of sleep brain wave patterns, only 50 percent of subjects who claimed they knew when they were about to nod off were actually able to predict it.

When you start to feel very sleepy, for example, while driving, you might change the temperature, turn on the radio, or roll down the window. Ultimately, you are still driving dangerous equipment while you are extremely sleepy; you are not overcoming your sleep debt. Your choices are (1) to avoid sleep debt in the first place, (2) stop driving when you are sleepy, (3) take a nap, and (4) use a stimulant like caffeine (provided you do not overdo it). Several new technologies to monitor and detect on-line alertness/performance are in place and being developed for driving. Although on-line alertness monitors do not prevent sleepiness, they can detect the problem and help avoid accidents.

Napping is another alternative. Its restorative power depends on the length of the nap, timing of the nap, type of sleep obtained during the nap, total amount of sleep debt prior to the nap, and what needs to occur when the nap is completed. Napping strategies to enhance shift work performance have been advised by some laboratory researchers but may be practical only on certain jobs.

A number of people have claimed that a brief nap of 10 minutes or so is refreshing and results in dramatically improved performance and vision. Researchers who have awakened brief-napping subjects in order to measure various psychomotor performance tasks have made the following conclusions:

- Napping can lead to improved performance, but the effect is not dramatic. Half an hour following a nap, performance will either remain on the same level or show slight improvement.
- Naps lasting 15 to 60 minutes increase alertness, but napping an additional hour has no added effect.
- The value of naps is affected by their timing in relation to circadian cycles. A nap at 8:00 P.M. may help the night shift worker on a subsequent shift but interfere with subsequent nocturnal sleep in a day worker.
- A sudden awakening from a nap is followed by decreased performance, a phenomenon called sleep inertia, which usually disappears within half an hour after awakening. Companies considering napping on the job as a coping strategy for workers will need to add in an extra 15- to 30-minute recovery period to maintain safety.

A nap prior to a night shift may be one instance when a person can "store" a sleep reserve to help maintain alertness at work during the 3:00 A.M.–4:00 A.M. slump. Two studies, one in Japan and one in Finland, found that shift workers who took daytime naps were more alert than non-nappers during the night shift, particularly toward the end of the shift. When we implemented what is called a rapid rotation 12-hour shift schedule (two 12-hour days, followed by 24 hours off, then two 12-hour nights, and then 4 days off) at Weyerhaueser in Prince Albert, Canada, the shift workers regularly napped in the afternoon prior to their first 12-hour night shift. Eighty-five percent of the crew reported taking a nap during the 24-hour break prior to the first night shift, and complaints of sleepiness were much less than on their old 8-hour schedule.

Performance

In several classic industrial studies conducted nearly 40 years ago, errors in meter readings at gas works peaked at night and between 2:00 P.M. and 4:00 P.M., and telephone operators connected calls much more slowly at night. Modern research and experience confirm that human performance, whether it's manual dexterity, arithmetic, reaction time, or cognitive reasoning, generally declines at night and in the afternoon about siesta time. In shift work operations where production is determined primarily by machines, night shift sleepiness will not have a large impact on productivity but may affect safety.

Some recent research suggests that type of performance may be optimal at different times. Short-term memorization may be better in the first 4 hours after a wakening for day workers. Shift workers on the night shift may be able to maintain performance on simple recognition tasks (yes-no, right-wrong decision making) by reducing their rate of activity. A refinery worker, for example, is more likely to skip taking a reading at 3:00 A.M. but does it correctly later. However, on ambiguous, judgment tasks, where decision making is more complex and there is no single right answer, increased performance errors at night are likely.

The Chernobyl accident occurred shortly after 1 A.M. when a team of engineers who had been on duty for 13 hours started a test at 11:00 P.M. and made a series of poor judgments. The shift workers entered erroneous data as the testing procedure was pushed along.

Fatigued workers' making poor decisions was a critical factor in probably the worst industrial accident: several hundred dead, unknown long-term health impact, and environmental damage estimated at over $300 billion.

Interaction of Factors I and II

Let's take a quick overview of where we are so far. Factors I and II are somewhat contradictory. Factor I suggests that if you want to adjust your body for the night shift, moving your biological clock so that your peak rhythm is at 3:00 A.M., you should work 365 consecutive night shifts without days off. Factor II, on the other hand, suggests that to prevent sleep debt, you should work only one or two shifts in a row, followed by a few days off. Unfortunately, there is no single answer to what is the healthiest and safest schedule. Some schedules are designed to maximize either Factor I or Factor II, while others seek a compromise. Furthermore, shift workers have different individual coping styles they are most comfortable with and likely to use, and these need to be taken into account in schedule design. If you design a circadian schedule (slowly rotating clockwise 8-hour) for tough-it-out shift workers (don't adjust; get through it), or a healthy rotating schedule for fixed shift workers, you could make their overall adjustment worse! By "slowly" I mean don't change shift hours (rotate) every day or every week—but maybe every *few* weeks.

I have worked with Olympic athletes and football players who are trying to move their peak performance to a new time zone. One-tenth of a second can be the difference between a gold medal, fame and fortune, or obscurity. As a rule, these athletes are committed to following unusual but healthy recommendations and directions. For example, one year the U.S. Olympic volleyball team had practices starting at 11:00 P.M., and a college football team had to be in the lobby of a Tokyo hotel at 4:00 A.M. to start calisthenics in order to move their peak performance rhythm for a game. Shift workers, however, are not this dedicated. They are not going to spend their time off adjusting their schedules for peak performance at work. Management has three basic obligations: (1) Set a schedule and work environment that makes it possible for the human body to adjust, (2) provide education to the employees and their families on how to make this adjustment, and (3) have a reasonable policy to deal with inevitable sleepiness that will occur. It's a little bit like being a travel agent. A travel agent can give you an itinerary for a trip that makes it easy for your body to adjust with plenty of breaks and gradual adjustments, or plan an itinerary guaranteed to provide maximum jet lag. The schedule is critical. However, even if you offer a healthy schedule, the traveler or shift worker can still end up fatigued and worn out by not following commonsense advice, such as trying to obtain at least 8 hours of sleep every day.

Shift Work and Safety

Which of the following four choices is the most frequent cause of ladder falls—one of the most common industrial accidents?

1. Work schedule (workload and work hours)
2. Personality (risk taking)
3. Job experience (history of previous on-the-job injuries)
4. Ladder usage (surface of set-up and quality of ladder)

The answer is 4. Factors related most directly to the accident are the best predictors of accidents. In comparisons to plants with high accident rates, low-accident-rate plants have better environmental conditions, including housekeeping and cleanliness, ventilation, lighting, and greater use of personal safety production equipment. In addition, strong management commitment to safety and ongoing annual safety training, effective hazard identification, employee involvement in the safety program, and integration of safety managers with operations managers are all hallmarks of good safety.

A number of other variables may affect the timing of occupational accidents. In a comprehensive study covering the years 1980–1984, researchers in Ontario, Canada, analyzed nearly 700,000 reportable accidents throughout the province. Peak periods for accidents occurred around noon, when plant activity, work demand, noise, and heat were at their maximum. (Perhaps a self-imposed pressure to get to lunch played a role as well.) There was a direct relationship between the number of accidents and level of plant activity (more accidents during day shift than night shift). The only exception was between 2:00 A.M. and 4:00 A.M., when there was a slight increase in accidents despite the decrease in activity.

Length of Shift

Determining which shift length is safest and most productive for your business requires analyzing many variables:

- Number of consecutive shifts worked
- Transportation time
- Shift start time
- Availability for sleeping at home between shifts
- Commuting distance and time
- Coping strategies of employees
- Ages of employees
- Type of work being done
- Whether job rotation is present
- Environmental conditions such as heating and lighting
- The work itself

Furthermore, the actual schedule may be very different from the master schedule. Companies on 12-hour shifts may be less likely to schedule excessive overtime than companies on 8-hour schedules, because they considered safety prior to implementing a longer shift length.

Additionally, there is no one right shift length. The numerous laboratory, field, and accident analysis studies for companies that work extended shifts, usually 10 or 12 hours, while maintaining a 40-hour workweek, have shown inconclusive results: both positive and negative effects. There is even a study done at the same location and using the same data but by two different research groups. One group said 12 hours were better for performance and alertness and safety; the other claimed 8 hours were better.

There are several reasons for the inconsistent findings: all 8-

hour and all 12-hour schedules are not the same; each facility is different; the motivation of the subjects varies; and which variable is measured has a bearing. We have seen operations where 15-minute shifts were too long (glass bottle inspectors) and others where 24 hours were too short (firemen who sleep on the job). My advice is to determine the type of work to be done and then measure performance. This will help you determine the best and safest shift length for your workers.

Human Factors

Most human errors in shift work operations are subtle and unpredictable, and they pass unnoticed. In the great majority of errors, the operations system provides feedback for the human to correct the operation, or the system itself may be self-correcting. Catastrophic failures usually are a consequence of multiple errors' cascading together out of control, with a series of poor interventions and wrong decision making. Often the interventions themselves cause the catastrophe. Commercial airlines, which necessitate an increasingly complex, complicated human-machine interface, report that two-thirds of all accidents are due to human error.

The integration of process equipment design and human capabilities is commonly referred to as human factors. Design engineers realize that the human variable of interaction with the system can make or break a system designed to avoid a catastrophic failure. Anyone who has spent time during working hours in a control room in a continuous process environment knows that there may be over 1,000 light and sound alarms that can be triggered under a wide capacity of operating conditions, including many that are still considered normal. Frequently shift workers shut off alarm signals, overriding the system design. In addition, lighting levels frequently are extremely low in control rooms, day and night, to reduce the glare (but inadvertently promoting fatigue). Whereas in the past management relied on shift workers to overcome design inefficiencies, control room designs are now being developed with the shift worker in mind.

Most design engineers, though, have not had training on shift work schedules, sleep research, and circadian rhythms, and no equipment or operation is 100 percent reliable. Shakespeare's admonition, "Some must watch while some must sleep," is more applicable today than ever before. Figure 3-4 shows some ways you can promote alertness at your 24-hour business.

Shift Work and Health

The most consistently documented health consequences of shift work are the inability to obtain enough good-quality sleep and excessive sleepiness during waking hours. The best way to study the health effects directly attributable to shift work is to compare workers in the same department: one group working day shift, the other either nights or rotating shift work. Assuming their seniority and age are equivalent, any impact would be clearly due to Factor I and Factor II. Only a few studies pinpoint the shift work problem in this fashion, however.

One recent study compared female shift workers in four large electronic factories in Singapore.* Factory conditions, including type of work (light assembly), were similar in each plant. The women made up groups of 8-hour day shift workers, 12-hour day shift workers, 12-hour night shift workers, and 12-hour rotating shift workers. No significant differences in hypertension (high blood pressure), health complaints, or absenteeism due to illness were found among the four groups. The 12-hour shift workers complained of more fatigue than the 8-hour workers, and the ones who rotated had a higher proportion of headache complaints. Overall, the research indicated no serious health problems for the 12-hour shift workers.

Longevity and Disease

Shift workers commonly believe that they have a shorter life span than those who do not work shifts, but there is no clear evidence to support this notion. In a carefully conducted study comparing approximately 4,000 shift workers with 4,000 day workers and 500

*O. Y. Chan, S. L. Gan, and M. H. Yeo, "Study on the Health of Female Electronics Workers on 12 Hour Shifts," *Occupational Medicine*, 1993.

Figure 3-4. Promoting alertness on the job.

P = Prevention D= Detection I = Intervention	
P	Get the right schedule.
P	Include human factors and shift worker input into your equipment/operations design.
D	Monitor alertness on line (e.g., the train stops when foot goes off the pedal or warning goes off if driver does not move wheel).
P	Replace sleepy workers with alert workers.
P	Use job rotation and cross training to prevent one worker's staying at a monotonous task.
D	Randomly throughout a shift, check alertness and performance by flashing a visual or cognitive test on the computer screen.
P, D, I	Simulate major accidents and incidents, and train shift work crews on interventions. What you do in practice is the best predictor of what you'll do during the real crisis.
P, I	Improve environmental conditions (heat, noise, exercise station). Dayton Power & Light, Mobil Oil, Southwestern Public Services, and Philadelphia Electric have put exercise stations in their control rooms.
P, I	Install bright lights.
P, I	Schedule regular rest breaks.
D, I	Alert supervisors to look for sleepy workers or operators.
I	Develop equitable disciplinary procedures.
I	Institute better day-off pattern.
P	Educate shift workers, supervisors, and management living well with shift work.
P	Develop an on-site physical training program.
D	Conduct a confidential survey (e.g., When are you the sleepiest? How often do you nod off?)
P, D, I	Acknowledge sleepiness is a problem.

ex-shift workers, no significant differences in mortality rates were noticed over a 10-year follow-up period. These results must be interpreted with some caution; had the 500 ex-shift workers remained in the shift work category and another 10 percent not dropped out of shift work for "medical reasons," the results might have been different. Several studies show that 20 percent of employees cannot tolerate night work, and 50 percent of shift workers who quit do so because of health reasons.

Older Workers

Older workers may encounter greater health difficulties on shift work because of several factors:

1. An increase in physiological sleep disorders among the older population (independent of work schedule) and, hence, more sleep deprivation.
2. Decrease in deep sleep with aging, resulting in loss of restorative sleep and more fatigue.
3. Greater propensity for awakening to noise due to less deep sleep.
4. Less flexible biological clocks and greater difficulty adjusting to schedule changes.
5. A tendency to have more health problems than younger workers.

Offsetting these negative trends is the finding that individuals who cannot tolerate shift work have usually dropped out by age 40; older shift workers are thus more likely to have developed a lifestyle and family support system compatible with shift work and are likely to be safe workers. They and their families accept shift work, and they are likely to have become experts in obtaining sufficient sleep. Furthermore, long-tenure shift workers may include more individuals whose biological clock naturally has more flexibility—the "shift worker survivor effect." Finally, a long-tenure shift worker has a good chance of seeing his or her organization change to a healthier schedule during his or her career and/or of finding a position on straight day shift.

Health Education for Shift Workers

There is no objective evidence that shift work educational programs alone can improve productivity, health and safety, and/or
morale, but education programs combined with a schedule change
have consistently been able to improve each of these key variables.
Information on such programs is widely available from organizations that give health, sleep, and circadian rhythm seminars. Readers interested in health education coping tips can also consult
"Scheduling ShiftWork" by Richard M. Coleman and Joseph
LaDou, in *Occupational Health and Safety*, 2d edition (Itasca, Ill.: National Safety Council, 1993).

Any educational program for shift workers should incorpo-
rate the following tips:

- Link advice to the specific schedule being worked. For example, 12-hour shift workers, 8-hour shift workers, fly in/fly
  out shift workers (see Chapter 5), rotating shift workers, and
  shift workers on unpredictable relief crews all need different
  advice. Furthermore, an unhealthy schedule is still an unhealthy schedule, even with the best advice.
- Include family members in the program. They will have
  questions and give advice based on their experience.
- It's better to give no advice than wrong advice. For example,
  no diet, foods, or drugs reset the circadian rhythm (see Figure 3-5).
- Time your program intelligently. Shift workers changing to
  a new schedule are looking for help and advice at that time.
  Most of the rest of the time, they develop their own methods
  of coping with their schedule and family and social life and
  they may not be open to change.

Probably just as important as shift work education is developing company policies for impaired sleepy shift workers. If employees are sleepy on the job, what will you do? Fire them? Tell them
to tough it out? Allow a nap? Send them home? Will you allow
employees to work 16-hour shifts, have quick comebacks, or work
excessive overtime without providing transportation? Make sure
you design policies that fit your situation and schedule.

Figure 3-5. Health tips.

Caffeine	When used in large quantities, may have a paradoxical effect and actually make the shift worker sleepier. Shift workers should use caffeine sparingly and strategically.
Alcohol	If used within 1 to 2 hours of bedtime, results in frequent awakening during sleep. If used during wake time hours, magnifies drowsiness if drinker is already sleep deprived.
Sleeping pills	Do not reset the biological clock, and can be addictive if not used properly.
Exercise	Does not play a major role in resetting the body clock, but regular exercise can increase deep, restorative sleep and improve alertness during working hours.
Diet	No convincing evidence that special diet helps adjustment to shift work. On the other hand, many shift workers have unhealthy diets.
Sanctioned napping	May make sense during shift work; is used in some industries.
Lighting	Can have an impact on biological rhythm and adjustment to shift work.
Melantonin	A naturally occurring hormone that responds to light and dark cycles and may have resetting properties. As yet has not been shown to reset biological clocks of shift workers.

Some European countries have developed nationwide policies for shift work. In France, shift lengths are a maximum of 10 hours a day, priority is given to shift workers with 10 years' shift work tenure to switch to day shift work, and low interest loans and/or subsidies are provided to soundproof and lightproof shift workers' houses. Some other European countries have limited night shift work to 7 hours, and companies may need governmental permits to work nights in the first place.

Conclusion

Circadian rhythm and sleep debt largely determine the degree of sleepiness and alertness for humans. For shift workers, the work schedule will be the key determinant. A good schedule, with awareness of circadian principles and frequent days off, enhanced by education and rational policies, will minimize health and safety problems. A bad schedule will create the opposite impact.

There are five basic scheduling design strategies for the health and safety circle. The first one is unhealthy; the other four are healthy:

1. *Zombie Schedules:* Schedules that pay no attention to scientific research, such as working 14 out of 15 days, 16-hour shifts, unpredictable and excessive overtime, or counterclockwise rotation, etc. These are often accompanied by outdated policies, such as, "You're fired if you fall asleep at work."

2. *Circadian Schedules:* Schedules that are designed to enhance the body's adjustment to each hour of the day. These will be 8-hour, rotating schedules, clockwise rotation, slowly rotating two or more workers, with a consolidated stretch of 5 to 10 consecutive nights.

3. *Factor II Schedules:* Schedules that are designed to minimize sleep debt but make no attempt to adjust circadian rhythms; for example, 8-hour rapid rotation with 24-hour breaks or 12-hour rapid rotation with a 24-hour break and 4 days off.

4. *Unbalanced Fixed Shifts:* The great majority of the workforce works either an 8-hour day shift or an 8-hour evening shift (3 P.M. to 11 P.M.).

5. *Anchor Sleep Schedules:* A compromise between Factor I and Factor II schedules. Usually worked with a block of 12-hour day shifts and then a block of 12-hour night shifts, with frequent days off during each block.

There are as well a wide variety of unique solutions, such as short (5- to 6-hour) night shifts and longer (8- to 10-hour) day and afternoon shifts, and part-time shifts.

If people are your most valuable asset, alert employees are even more valuable. A reasonable master schedule, a reasonable actual schedule, education for employees, and policies to accommodate sleepy workers will keep you operating safely and out of the courtroom. In the future, technologies such as lighting, pharmaceutical intervention, robots, and on-line alertness monitoring may also overcome the human limitations to operating day and night.

4

Employee Desires

If a business is to run effectively around the clock, employees must support the schedule. Otherwise, morale and productivity will suffer, and there will be a constant exodus of trained employees from key shift work positions, with costly results. Imagine the opposite situation. At Corning, in Wilmington, North Carolina, the employees were so happy with their new schedule that the plant manager received numerous write-in votes for union president. The impact of happy shift workers coming to work every day can be so dramatic that they eclipse the cost savings and health and safety benefits.

A Simple Test for Schedule Satisfaction

Shift workers' schedule satisfaction can be determined by asking, "Have you considered bidding out of your shift work job in the past 12 months?" In 1985, 70 percent of the shift workers we met with said yes. In 1994, only 45 percent said yes. (This question is asked prior to our company's making a schedule change). This positive trend over the last 10 years may be due in part to the growth of better schedules and the realization that shift work can offer a positive lifestyle. Nevertheless, of those who have considered getting out of shift work, 75 percent indicate the reason is to get a better work schedule. Only 13 percent would bid out to get a better job, and 12 percent for better pay (Figure 4-1).

Generally the work schedule is about the most important employment issue for a shift worker. If you're a Monday through Friday day worker, imagine the response of your spouse, children, friends, and relatives to the news that starting today you'll be

Figure 4-1. Workers' responses to the question: "Have you considered bidding out of shift work in the past year?"

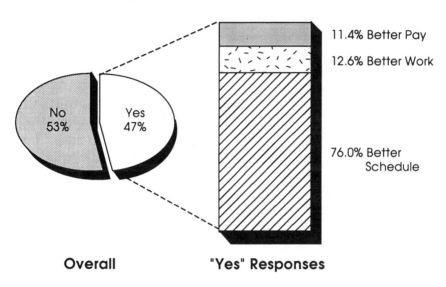

11.4% Better Pay

12.6% Better Work

76.0% Better Schedule

No 53%   Yes 47%

Overall   "Yes" Responses

Source: CCG Shiftworker Normative Database.

working night shifts for the next 10 years, with 13 weekends off each year plus 2 weeks' vacation. Now imagine giving them the following news: For the next 10 years you'll be having an extra 90 days off per year, a 10 percent pay increase, 10 weeks of vacation per year, and twenty-six 3-day weekends off, but you'll need to work 20 weekends a year and five night shifts each month. Your family might ask, "Why haven't you signed up already?" A shift work schedule that is better than a traditional Monday through Friday, 9 A.M.–5 P.M. schedule can solve most employee desire issues.

Opportunities to bid out of shift work are usually limited. Few companies have openings for 47 percent of their workforce to move into day jobs every year, although opportunities may exist across several years or a decade. Many employees who take shift work jobs have no intention of making it their life's work and will "bid out," or try to transfer to day work, as soon as possible. To combat this loss of trained personnel from the evening and night shifts, many companies have instituted restrictions that employees may bid out of shift work only after working with a company for six years. Such restrictions can hurt morale if the schedule is deemed very undesirable by shift workers. In many established 24-hour businesses, shift workers move from department to department or job to job just to avoid onerous schedules or to find better ones. This process may work well for employees who "make it" but can leave those who are stuck behind resentful. And this has a negative effect on the business. One Mead Johnson plant spent a half-million dollars each year to retrain its 200-person workforce in an effort to accommodate employees' constant job bid changes. Implementing schedules that employees find attractive can eliminate these problems. At some locations we have observed several electricians and maintenance employees volunteering to go from day work into shift work positions without extra pay; the attraction of the new schedule was that it provided thirty-one 5-day weekends each year.

Employees' Primary Concerns

If you are considering changing schedules at your facility and ask shift workers what type of schedule they want, the typical first reaction is, "Don't touch my pay and benefits." Initially many shift workers view any suggestion of a schedule change as a potential loss of something they currently have. If there's a high level of distrust at a facility, or if there are "money schedules" in place (that is, unattractive work schedules that have been "improved" with financial incentives), there will be greater negative reaction initially. Shift workers at one paper mill work 14 out of 15 days, changing shift every week. This schedule has an unhealthy backward rotation (nights to afternoons to days), and there are only 13 weekends off per year; however, Sunday is paid at double time, and time and one-half is paid for working any scheduled day off, for working over 8 hours in a day, or for working over 40 hours in a week. Employees can easily increase their wages by 50 percent by pyramiding overtime. As a result, although this schedule is considered unattractive by most shift workers worldwide and it is difficult on the body, the acceptance level at the mill remains high.

But even if the trust level is high at your facility and you do not have money schedules in place, there may be an initial resistance to change. Work hours have a tremendous impact on employees' financial situation, personal life, outside interests, social life, and family life. Any change can upset a delicate balance (probably unseen by the employer, who does not know the employees' outside world) that may have taken years of expert juggling to achieve. Employees become experts at making a bad schedule work, so the initial reaction against change may be resistance even when the current schedule is disliked. They have mastered the system on bidding, vacation selection, overtime, sick policy, managing family-social activities, or possibly a second job.

In 1993, forty angry guards closed down the Louvre in Paris while protesting plans to change their shift schedule when the new Richelieu wing opened in November. The guards were working ten nights a month, from 6:00 P.M. to 9:00 A.M., and were able to group their shifts together in order to have long stretches of time off. The museum was planning to increase the night staff and limit flexibility in individual schedules. The protest cost the Louvre about $50,000 in lost revenues.*

If a high trust level exists at your facility and your prospective schedule will not have an impact on pay and benefits, the next issue that usually pops up for employees is overtime. Some employees are willing to work every available overtime opportunity; others never volunteer for overtime, preferring time off. The majority of shift workers fall somewhere in between; they would like to see overtime opportunities always available but have the luxury of choosing at their convenience when to work it. It's not unusual for a manufacturing plant to work excessive overtime during the winter months without employee complaints, only to find a disgruntled workforce complaining about too much overtime during the summer even when the actual overtime level has remained constant.

When pay, benefits, and overtime are not going to change and

*"Guards Close Down Louvre," *The New York Times*, September 30, 1993.

trust level is high, it is easier to find out what employees' actual scheduling desires are. This open-ended question usually works: "What is the primary benefit you'd like to see from changing schedules?" Over the years, we have found that the answers fall into four major categories: (1) better time off, (2) better health and alertness, (3) more predictable schedule, or (4) increased overtime. Figure 4-2 shows the relative ranking of each of these issues, circa 1995.

Issue 1: Time Off

It makes sense that employees who must cover nights, weekends, and holidays should have the same amount of time off as, or maybe more than, Monday through Friday day workers, but historically this has not been the case. Day workers in the United States are generally scheduled for 2,080 annual hours (52 weeks × 40 hours) but actually work only 1,840 because they get 5 sick days, 10 holidays, and 3 weeks of vacation and work little overtime. Twenty-four-hour shift workers are typically scheduled for 2,184 annual hours (52 weeks × 42 hours) and work all 2,184 hours because

Figure 4-2. Employees' desired benefits from changed schedules, circa 1995.

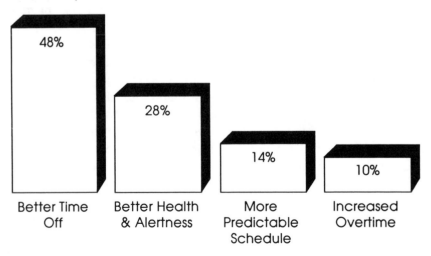

| Better Time Off | Better Health & Alertness | More Predictable Schedule | Increased Overtime |

they work through holidays and must cover each other's sickness and vacation. The difference between 2,184 and 1,840 is roughly 340 hours, and since shift workers normally work more overtime than day workers, the actual difference is closer to 400 hours—equivalent to 10 extra 40-hour workweeks a year, or 10 fewer weeks off per year.

Time off for shift workers, moreover, is more likely to come at the wrong time. One shift worker with 36 years of tenure never received a complete weekend off until his thirty-seventh year of work. Another loyal employee could not get off for his daughter's graduation; a father never saw his son pitch in Little League. Whereas most family and social life is scheduled on weekends, Saturday and Sunday in a 24-hour, 7-day business may only represent two-sevenths (28 percent) of the days off. Furthermore, a day worker who misses a day of work can catch up the next day because the workload is often discretionary. In shift work, the coverage is needed today, so it's much more difficult to come in late or take a day off for a graduation or doctor's appointment.

Time off may also be of poor quality. Many shift work schedules provide prime time off only after a stretch of night shifts. It's not unusual for shift workers to spend half of the long weekend break trying to adjust the body clock to daytime hours instead of enjoying the free time. If the time off is infrequent, shift workers may be bombarded with a list of duties that have been put on hold pending their time off. Male shift workers sometimes call these days off "honey do days" as in "Honey, do this" and "Honey, do that." Female shift workers with children and/or husbands typically find that *all* of their "time off" becomes taken up with other duties around the house.

The combination of these three time-off problems—less of it, wrong time, and poor quality—can severely disrupt family-social life.

Solutions

For shift workers the term *better days off* has several meanings. One of the most important is obtaining enough time off. With traditional shift schedules covering 24 hours per day, 365 days per year, only 45 percent of all shift workers get enough time off; with Best

Cost Schedules, 88 percent of shift workers surveyed report they get enough time off.

The simplest calculation for "better days off" is the total number of days off a year. Other issues are number of weekends off and number of total calendar days of vacation. A day worker who utilizes 40 hours of vacation (1 week off) receives 9 calendar days off: 5 weekdays plus 4 weekend days (2 on each side of the weekdays). A shift worker's vacation is largely a function of the schedule and vacation policy. In some schedules, 56 vacation hours may result in only 10 calendar days off, whereas in other schedules, 40 vacation hours can mean 14 calendar days off, and in yet another, 24 vacation hours will yield 7 calendar days off. Figure 4-3 shows employee satisfaction ratings of time off on an old schedule and a new one. This information is from our database of thousands of shift workers at hundreds of companies on hundreds of different schedules who changed to hundreds of new schedules.

Another important element of better days off is flexibility. The ability for shift workers to schedule time off when they need it is critical to the success of a schedule. It allows the shift worker to maintain a predictable schedule outside of work that matches the schedules of their family, friends, classes, teammates, and others. Remember that their schedule is already contrary to the majority of the population who work only days, Monday through Friday. From management's perspective, as long as the right skills are at the right place, at the right time, at the right cost, it shouldn't matter which individual is on duty. As a general principle, employees should be able to trade shifts, which allows shift workers more flexibility than day workers, the equivalent of having unlimited (no-cost) personal days. As a result, shift workers can find time to attend school, take a family member to the doctor, or play golf when they need to.

With this degree of flexibility must come responsibility. If employees cannot sustain coverage without overtime, trading is restricted. At one mining and chemical operation, the employees cross trained themselves in order to maximize their ability to trade days off. The supervisor literally did not know who would be coming to work until a few minutes before the shift began. Although this may sound like chaos, these are the same individuals who op-

Figure 4-3. Satisfaction ratings of time off—old and new schedules.

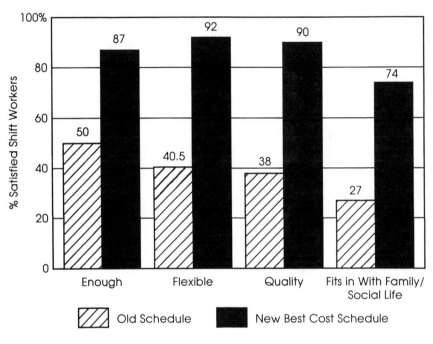

Source: CCG Normative Data Base.

erate millions of dollars of capital equipment every night while management is at home.

In some companies shift workers have developed their own flexible arrangements unbeknown to senior management, so be careful about taking away a system that is working well. On the other hand, be wary of violations of overtime policies. At a public utility in Florida, seven years of employee-driven shift trades suddenly became expensive when a disgruntled employee pointed out to city officials that although shift workers didn't put overtime on their time cards, back pay with interest was legally due.

Because of federal overtime rules, most shift trades must be completed in the same week, making the system more limited. In countries where overtime can be averaged over a cycle, the trades can be completed over several weeks.

Shift trading can be facilitated or hindered by the master schedule. You can design a schedule that facilitates trading of shifts without a single person working overtime, but in most U.S. companies, shift trading is onerous for employees. In the common "Southern Swing," for example (a 4-crew, weekly rotating schedule, shown in detail in Chapter 5), shift trades inevitably involve one employee's working a double shift (16 hours straight) or quick comeback (8 hours on, 8 hours off, 8 hours on). In other schedules, shift trading flexibility (without overtime) is built in as a key schedule design feature. Trades are made with a co-worker working the same hours so there are no double shifts or quick comebacks.

The quality of time off is an important feature of shift schedules. Each employee defines quality somewhat differently. Before implementation of Best Cost Schedules, 38 percent of the shift workers we surveyed reported having quality time off; after implementation it increased to 90 percent. By comparison, only 62 percent of Monday through Friday day shift workers in our database report their schedules give adequate quality time off. (For example, day workers rarely get a weekday off or a built-in 5-day weekend.) The shift worker who is working a Best Cost Schedule rates his quality time off better than day workers.

Quality time for most employees means having blocks of time off in the right sequence to fit their outside needs. Normally, this means getting weekends off, but this is not always the case. At 3M Company, in Decatur, Alabama, the shift schedule was popular because it provided maximum weekdays off. Fishing was one of the employees' major time-off activities, and weekends on the lakes and rivers were too crowded. Similarly, working with Con Edison in New York City, we found that workers said that weekends off were not critical to them. Living in a crowded metropolitan area, it was more valuable to maximize weekdays off.

The pattern of time off is also critical. One refinery in a rural area of Pennsylvania had a schedule that built in 13 consecutive days off every 5 weeks. It was too long in the winter months but appropriate during the better-weather months. It is possible to design schedules with different day-off patterns for different seasons of the year. In metropolitan and suburban locations, employees may desire frequent, short breaks (2 or 3 days off at a time), whereas in more remote locations, employees often need a week-long break to travel to home, friends, family, city, or civilization. Talking to your shift workers about their needs will help you pinpoint their specific desires. (I gave up a long time ago trying to figure out what pattern any given group of shift workers might prefer. We know what the average shift worker wants, but we've never met the average shift worker.)

Another way to evaluate an employee's schedule is to ask how well it fits with his or her family-social life. Companies that call us in for help on average have only 27 percent of their shift workers indicating the current schedule fits their family social life. After implementing a Best Cost Schedule, the average is 74 percent. However, we will never get 100 percent to agree that the schedule meets everyone's family and social needs because shift work is still shift work. Even with Monday through Friday straight day work, only 68 percent of workers indicate their schedule fits with their outside life. In general, the more time off there is, the more flexibility for trading, the more predictability, and the more the schedule was designed with employee input, the greater are the chances of meeting an employee's family and social life needs.

But even when the change is for the best, shift workers can be suspicious. Listen to the experience of a single shift worker who helped make a difference for hundreds of co-workers. Mac Robertson is a 36-year-old shift worker from Tulsa, Oklahoma, who works in the shipping department of a large manufacturing plant that is open 365 days a year, 24 hours a day. He described the schedule he worked at the plant when he was in his mid-twenties as "a 7-day swing schedule":

We started on graveyard (11 P.M.–7 A.M.) and worked 7 of those in a row, got 2 days off, then worked 7 afternoon shifts (3 P.M.–1 P.M.) with 1 day off, and then 7 day shifts (7 A.M.–3 P.M.) with 4 days off. Shift work wasn't good for my marriage, and it wasn't good for my sleep. When I rotated into the day shift sequence, I called that "hell week" because I could not sleep at night. My wife was a counselor with a master's degree in psychology. She tried different things—relaxation tapes and things like that—and nothing worked. We didn't know at that time that rotating backward was really what was causing my problems.

On his own, Mac tracked down Coleman Consulting Group and after 12 months of gathering information and keeping the issue alive, convinced his managers to pursue a consultation, which eventually led to an entire change process.

Some of my co-workers were excited about it and open to change; some of them were not. There was some positive reaction, and there were some very negative reactions. I'm sorry it wasn't something that management started. Because they didn't initiate it, I think there were some people in management who really gave me a hard time.

Basically, the consultant who came in educated us. We didn't even know that there were so many alternatives. After this process of education, we were given a lot of different options to look at as far as schedules were concerned and narrowed it down. Then we took a vote on it by department through the entire plant, and then after it was passed, it was implemented about two or three months later.

The people who had been positive about it throughout the change process remained so. The people who had been negative about it through the change process changed their minds after they actually got on the schedule.

The new schedule has 12-hour shifts, but more days off.

Before, my existence was work, eat, and sleep. Now I have time to enjoy life. And I don't have any more problems sleeping at night. That absolutely came to a halt. I feel like I'm living now. Before it was simply existence. I took my little boy to the doctor yesterday, got back home, and went to my little girl's T-ball game. Before, I had just one weekend a month; I have two now, plus time during the week to watch my little boy instead of having him in day care. It's a lot better. Also, I'm a hunter and a fisherman. I take four or five hunting or fishing trips a year without using my vacation. I feel better physically and mentally.

I would choose this schedule over a straight day job. Recently I had an opportunity to work straight days for 6 weeks and I found myself missing shift work. I didn't think that I would ever say that.

I think that in order to solve the problems with shift work, you have to make it more attractive than straight day work.

I'll tell you what's happened to me. I was at the mall around Christmas time and a woman came up to me and thanked me for what I did—for changing the schedule over there—because it made her life with her husband, who worked there, a lot better.

There were a couple of my co-workers in a different department who did not want to have anything whatsoever to do with this shift change. They didn't vote for it, and they really didn't have much to do with me until they had been on the new schedule for about 2 weeks. That's all it took—2 weeks. One of them came up to me and said that he really liked it; it was a lot easier than he thought it would be and a lot better than what we were doing before. He pretty much apologized for his attitude before. They have both been really friendly to me ever since.

Issue 2: Health and Alertness

Shift workers consistently rank health and alertness as their second most important concern, after time off. In Chapter 3 we looked at some of the research on the impact of schedules on health and safety and alertness.

Shift workers can have a big impact on their own health and alertness by their regular health practices. Six key health practices have been shown to be good predictors of health and longevity. Take this little quiz:

	Yes	*No*
I am the proper weight for my height, not over-weight.	☐	☐
I eat breakfast every day.	☐	☐
I sleep 7 to 8 hours each 24-hour day.	☐	☐
I am a nonsmoker.	☐	☐
I am a nondrinker (or have two or fewer alcoholic drinks on occasions when I do drink).	☐	☐
I exercise often and regularly.	☐	☐
Total the number of *yes* answers:_____		

On average, day workers follow 4.1 of these practices, shift workers only 2.8. Despite increased awareness of the risks, 31 percent of American adults are overweight (defined as 20 percent above desirable weight), according to the U.S. National Center for Health Statistics. Obesity has been linked to cancer, cardiovascular disease, diabetes, and gallbladder disease. The root cause, according to experts, is a sedentary lifestyle and abundance of fatty food.

Among shift workers the problem is worse: overall, 49 percent report being overweight even though only 34 percent eat breakfast regularly. Most likely the lack of consistent meal schedule and availability of healthy foods at all hours contributes to the high obesity rate. In addition, shift workers have a fairly sedentary lifestyle; only 38 percent report exercising regularly. Many shift workers complain that their work schedules make it nearly impossible to maintain an exercise regimen.

As a group, shift workers are fairly healthy on two of the other key health practices. Sixty-three percent are nonsmokers, and 65 percent are nondrinkers or drink in moderation. The major breakdown is in lack of sleep; only 37 percent get at least 7 to 8 hours per day on a regular basis, which in turn results in excessive sleepiness. Thirty percent of shift workers nod off or fall asleep during activities on days off.

Issue 3: Predictability

Fourteen percent of all workers say that obtaining a more predictable schedule is their primary concern. Companies that schedule overtime at the last minute (either on days off or by extensions of workdays) create a tremendous disruption to family and social life plans, which may have been on the calendar for weeks. It's one thing for a parent to tell a child that they cannot schedule a camping trip this summer; it's another matter to postpone or cancel a planned trip one day before leaving because of a change in work schedules.

Some companies have an archaic seniority system that builds unpredictable scheduling for the entire workforce into the master schedule. At one oil refinery if you are the number two employee in seniority, getting ready on Wednesday for your upcoming 3-day weekend (employees only get 7 full weekends off per year), and you find out on Thursday that the number one seniority person will be taking sick days instead of working the upcoming weekend, your schedule slot changes from slot number two to slot number one. All of a sudden you do not have a weekend off. You have Tuesday and Wednesday off, and if you're lucky you'll get a shot at another weekend in 7 weeks. This system cascades all the way down to the most junior person. The result is a totally unpredictable schedule, every week, for every employee.

Other shift work systems have designated relief operators who fill in for sickness and vacation. Knowing your life will be chaotic is actually a form of predictability, and there are some shift workers who prefer the relief slot. Typically they work many stretches of night shift during the summer (peak vacation time) and many day shifts with a fair number of weekends off the remainder of the year. Most problems of unpredictability can be solved or reduced with better schedules that match the actual workload and the shift workers provide improved self-regulating coverage.

Issue 4: Overtime

Ten percent of shift work employees select increased overtime as their primary scheduling goal. These tend to be the "overtime

hogs" whose financial situation makes them completely dependent on overtime. (One shift worker making $7.50 an hour was
very unhappy when his company added 25 percent more workers
to reduce overtime. He told us, "I know it's not your fault, but I
need that overtime just for my family to survive.") Other overtime
hogs are in a good financial position but have fixed payments, a
second mortgage, or a third car to maintain. Thirty-one percent of
shift workers depend on overtime for their regular personal fi-
nances.

Figure 4-4 shows the acceptance level by shift workers of overtime levels at different plants. At plants with no overtime at all we
find a 33 percent approval rating, while at plants with more than
20 overtime hours per week only 16 percent approve. Facilities
with seven and a half hours of overtime per week obtain the highest satisfaction level by shift workers, 75 percent.

On average, shift workers prefer a greater than 40-hour workweek. Furthermore, two-thirds of shift workers would prefer the

Figure 4-4. Overtime approval rating of shift workers worldwide.

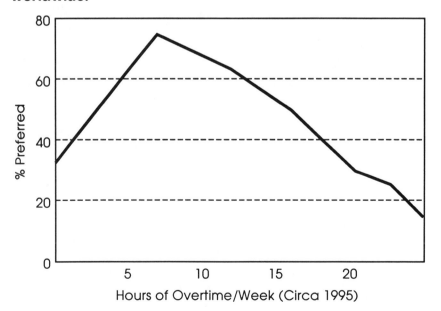

Hours of Overtime/Week (Circa 1995)

overtime to be built in to the master schedule for predictability. It is possible to develop schedules with any amount of built-in overtime, without disrupting days off.

In our consulting experience we have encountered a number of unusual overtime situations. A textile manufacturer near Melbourne, Australia, has a standard workweek of 35 hours. However, employees were actually working six 12-hour shifts each week with Sundays off, or 72 hours. This schedule had been in place for nearly 2 years and became widely accepted by union, management, and shift workers. Management's implementation of a new schedule reducing the employee workweek to 56 hours was met with extreme dissatisfaction. Even though overtime was still high at 23 hours per week, it was viewed as a take-away. If employees become accustomed to any level of predictable, continuous overtime, reductions can severely disrupt morale, especially among those financially dependent on it.

In most companies different departments have different overtime patterns, and the employees manage to find their way to the department that meets their needs. At a manufacturing plant in Indiana, only employees who guaranteed they would work any overtime shift offered, without restriction, could work in one particular department. Many shift workers in this department had worked 365 days, with no days off, with gross earnings nearly triple the equivalent straight time rate. Not only did the employees work every day, they also worked an enormous number of double shifts, covering vacancies on other shifts in other departments. Most of these extreme overtime hogs were the most senior employees at the large facility. Even the union president confided to me that these employees were addicted to overtime: "They don't need the extra money but they wouldn't know what to do with a day off." Extreme overtime hogs tend to be the most vocal supporters of the current schedule (even though they are not working the master schedule) and most resistant to change. Since they have the overtime system down pat, any change is a threat to them.

In a Best Cost Schedule, there will always be some overtime. Since idle time is so expensive, it's less costly to cover unexpected last-minute vacancies with overtime. In addition, with the high benefit load many operations carry, a small amount of built-in overtime may be appropriate, as well. For health and safety reasons, however, it is often prudent to place a reasonable limit on overtime. If a large amount of overtime needs to be worked in a short time—for example, during a power plant's planned outage—design a schedule that still provides frequent days off. Employees can work 4 days on and 2 days off while averaging a 56-hour workweek.

The Changing Workforce and Schedules

The American workforce is changing, and shift work schedules need to change as well. There are more females, single parents, and individuals with primary responsibility for children or aged parents entering the workforce. Employees who cannot meet their basic family obligations are unlikely to remain in your organization, despite good pay, benefits, and employee involvement. A good schedule will help; a bad schedule can be the breaking point.

Available leisure time is shrinking, partly because of speeded-up communication, transportation, and information. We can now do more in each 24-hour period and as a result actually have less available free time than 20 years ago. Americans have reported a decline in leisure time of up to one-third since the 1970s. Simultaneously, the average number of hours worked per year has increased by 100 hours for both exempt and nonexempt employees over the past 20 years. Predictably, time for eating, sleeping, and family has declined, while stress has increased.

Among the millions of Americans who fall victim to the shortage of time, the most heavily affected group is women. Studies of household labor from 1890 to today have shown that despite dramatic technology improvements, hours of household work have remained constant. Two nationwide studies found that employed American women work close to 85 hours per week, including their jobs and home-child duties.

Overtime has been increasing since the start of the 1990s as companies downsize and focus on productivity improvements. With more workers in lower-paying service jobs and the decrease in high-paying manufacturing jobs, overtime will likely remain high in the foreseeable future. Increased overtime also makes financial sense because benefit loading costs (i.e. fringe benefits) doubled from an average of 17 percent in 1955 to 35 to 40 percent in 1994. There are not too many predictions that the rates will decrease. The United Auto Workers estimated that overtime in one recent year alone could have been converted to employing 88,000 laid-off workers. It's a tough quandary for union leaders, who want to preserve jobs but also please their senior members, who rely on overtime to maintain the standard of living they have become accustomed to.

Employees in Germany, Sweden, and Australia work fewer hours than Americans; in Korea and Japan they work more. In Japan, overtime hours have been at record highs in the past 10 years, leading to *Karoshieitakes* ("death by overwork"). Nonindustrialized, emerging nations generally work more hours. The determination of basic hours, vacations and holidays, and overtime versus leisure time differs according to legislation, culture, policies, and economic conditions.

Despite the increase in productivity in American businesses over the last 40 years, the dream of a 4-day workweek is just that—a dream—at least for day workers. But there is good news for shift workers who desire more pay and increased time off. With the right extended shift schedules, it is possible for them to have it both ways: They can get their overtime (as much as 20 percent) and still have more days off than a 35-hour-per-week German employee.

Shift Work and Families

Shift work can make or break a family. In studies carried out in the 1970s and early 1980s, shift workers had a higher rate of divorce than day workers. As divorce rates have crept up for all workers, the difference from day workers is now less noticeable. In some cases, shift work can help marriage. On the other hand, occasionally a new schedule that dramatically improves time off can backfire and result in spouses' having too much time together, which can unmask problems. Shift work, in other words, can hide a bad marriage.

Choosing a career in shift work is based on a number of inter-
acting variables. For some families, the shift worker is the primary
breadwinner; in most cases, though, both adults are working, as
Figure 4-5 indicates. When we asked fathers the primary reason
they work nontraditional hours, 69 percent said the job demands
it. Married mothers said the primary reason is for better child care
arrangements (42 percent). Therefore, married mothers are more
likely to seek out a shift work position to enhance their family
schedule while adding extra income. Changing the schedules of
such workers must be undertaken carefully, or turnover can sky-
rocket. Unmarried mothers report that demands of the job (47 percent) and better child care (22 percent) were the key factors for
choosing shift work. When you ask families to identify the impact
of shift work, it's critical to refer to a specific schedule. Don't con-

Figure 4-5. Shift worker spouse profile.

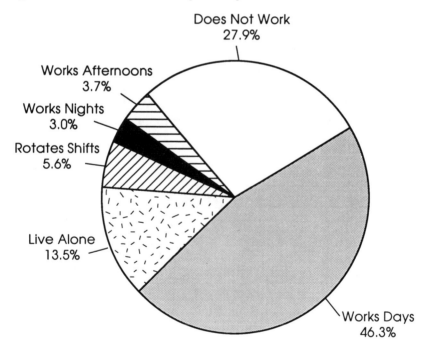

Spouse = Husband/Wife/Person You Live With

fuse families' reaction to shift work in general with the reaction to the one schedule they are familiar with and cope with every day. Recently an Australian university researcher reported that more than 60 percent of the women in Australia's coal mining communities reported negative effects from a 7-day schedule and went on to recommend that 7-day schedules should be restricted. The same year, at a facility in the United States, we found that 78 percent of the shift workers' families on a Best Cost 7-day schedule were *satisfied* with the work schedule. It is not that 7-day schedules are a problem; it was the Australian miners' 7-day schedule that was the problem. Below is a comparison of the schedule the miners' wives complained about, and the one implemented in the U.S. mining operation.

Australian Miners' *7-Day Roster*	*U.S. (Best Cost)* *7-Day Schedule*
91 days off per year	188 days off per year
13 weekends off per year	31 weekends off per year
Always work 7 days in a row	Work no more than 4 days in a row
40–42 work hours per pay week	40–42 work hours per pay week
39 shift rotations per year	10 shift rotations per year
8-hour shift length	8 and 12-hour shift length
Longest break is 4–5 days	Longest break is 8 days
5 weeks of leave	10 weeks of leave

The key is to remember that shift work is not in itself "bad." The employee and family perception of the schedule is what counts. Bad schedules will be bad for employees and their families; good schedules can make shift work an attractive lifestyle. It's hard to guess what feature an employee will find most important. The following comments are from three shift workers who changed to the same new schedule:

"I have more quality time off with my family than before, only having to work 3 or 4 days at a time. The long weekend is great."

"We always have at least 2 days off each week. It provides us
with having different days off and being able to plan family
activities."

"I can spend more time with my family. My sleeping habits
are better, and my mind and body feel better. My body han-
dles the shift change from days to nights better."

Many women who are part of a two-income family, as well as unmarried women with small children, are now working shift work.
Child care is a critical issue for these employees, especially if the
company is considering changing schedules. We have found that
over 80 percent of shift workers find a way to maintain child care
with traditional resources such as family, extended family, babysit-
ters, and daytime day care. A smaller percentage may utilize
around-the-clock child care. Since most 24-hour businesses are not
experts in the child care business, it is usually better for companies
to stay out of that field and help subsidize local child care centers
that are willing to extend their hours.

What do children think of living in a shift work family? The
opinions vary by age and the family's schedule or the child's own
schedule. One 11-year-old girl from California, whose dad is a police officer working rotating 8-hour shifts, said, "I can see my dad
every day. I just have to be quiet when he's sleeping." Other children who are dropped off at day care centers at odd hours have
complaints such as fatigue, missing after-school activities, and difficulty having time alone.

Other Shift Worker Needs

Shift workers have other needs besides child care. Scheduling policies
should also take into account important outside activities such as
religion, education, community services, sports, and so on. In fact, 10
to 20 percent of your workforce may be in school. Many companies
support further education to help increase technical skills. They can
design a shift schedule to make it easier for employees to attend
classes, while maintaining full operational coverage at the work site.
Another solution is to bring education to the plant. SEH America in
Vancouver, Washington, has educational trailers at the plant site, and

the local community college offers courses with schedules that match shift schedules.

Shift Worker Schedule Preferences

Whenever you consider changing schedules, a number of family and social issues will arise. Define the particular problems, and determine how many employees are really affected. Then:

1. Design schedules that minimize the problems.
2. Communicate the new reduced scope of the problem, and allow shift workers time to change their outside arrangements.
3. Allow reasonable, flexible shift trading.
4. Provide assistance to employees who still have problems. Without addressing these concerns, shift work employees may turn down a better schedule because they cannot rearrange their life.

When I am trying to guess out which schedule employees will like at a specific operation, or even department, I try to remember the following principles before I make my prediction:

1. I have never met the average shift worker yet.
2. Shift work is still shift work.
3. There's a bias toward a schedule similar to the current one.
4. There's a big difference between looking at a schedule and working it.
5. Shift workers make decisions in mysterious ways, defying all predictions.

Do shift workers in different geographical locations prefer one type of schedule? No. We have found that whether we are in Australia, South America, Africa, Europe, Asia, or North America, whether we're working with computer programmers in California or tribes in Papua New Guinea, shift workers are more alike than they are different. Schedules that are predictable; provide high pay; maximum time off, quality time off, and flexibility of time off; are consistent; and match their family and social life are accepted by shift workers. Schedules that do not meet these criteria are disliked and have a negative impact on employee morale and turnover. Although there may be specific trends within a country or geographic region, this is usually a result of lack of exposure to alternative schedules. Often when a schedule is new to a geographic area, a number of nearby companies immediately copy the new "solution."

Each shift worker sees the schedule in his or her personal context. Some even prefer nights. Carolyn Peterson, a registered nurse who works in labor and delivery at Marin General Hospital near San Francisco, has worked a lot of different schedules in the past 12 years:

> I started working night shifts specifically so that I could take classes during the day; then I grew attached to the shifts and the people I was working with. I felt a loyalty to that shift and camaraderie, and I just never left. It was difficult working night shifts and trying to attend classes during the day, and it made studying and thinking more difficult, but I managed to get through it all.
>
> Among those of us who work night shifts to keep the hospital running, there is a certain martyrdom quality that we feel that nobody else can understand. We stay up when nobody else is willing to stay up; we take more care of the patients; there is nobody else in the hospital to help us. Physicians prefer to stay at home for long periods of time during the nights, so we end up doing more procedures that physicians might be doing during the day. We feel as if we are part of something like the special services in the army. We're hot stuff, and a lot of us like to work night shifts for that reason.
>
> Sometimes people work night shifts because it's convenient for their family. I work with a lot of single moms who prefer to spend time with their children in the evening, so they work nights and sleep during the day while their kids are at school. Then they are home to send them off to school instead of having to be at work at 7:00 A.M.
>
> One thing that I do notice is that people who work

nights don't realize after a period of time that they are getting tired and burned out. Once they transfer to another shift and start sleeping regularly at night, they notice a difference in their attitude.

Critical Issues for Schedule Preferences

Fixed Shifts

In Chapter 2 we examined fixed shifts from the business perspective, noting that they were advantageous for unbalanced workloads but with disadvantages of skill imbalance, communication difficulties, and poor teamwork. In Chapter 3 I pointed out that fixed shifts are advantageous for health and safety if night shift staffing is proportionally low and bright lighting or shorter shift lengths are utilized.

Employee opinion of fixed shifts is somewhat different. In most locations with a history of fixed shifts, the employees are very supportive of the system. Either a majority of the employees are on the shift they prefer, or there is light at the end of the tunnel: Shift workers are able to transfer to their preferred shift in a reasonable time frame. Fixed shifts can make it easier to plan family life, arrange child care, attend classes, and so on. In fact, the most stable schedule is fixed shifts with fixed days off, which is what most day workers have (9:00 A.M.–5:00 P.M., Monday through Friday with Saturday and Sunday off).

Organizations with a history of rotating shifts have the opposite prejudice. At Pennsylvania Power & Light, in Allentown, Pennsylvania, I met with union and management and suggested that we look at some fixed shift options. The union leadership didn't want to listen: "We're not interested in fixed shifts. They are not fair." End of discussion. Pennsylvania Power & Light's power stations have a long tradition of working rotating schedules. Rotating schedules are accepted, and fixed shifts don't fit in.

Fixed shifts are a winner for individuals on their preferred shift but a major problem for those stuck on a less desired shift with little hope of transferring in the foreseeable future. Stress will increase on the shift worker until something gives—family, personal life, or job.

Worldwide, shift workers prefer fixed shifts if they can get on the day shift, whether they work an 8-hour day or a 12-hour day (Figure 4-6). Twenty-four percent of those who work 8-hour shifts prefer rotating schedules (either because they prefer rotating schedules, which typically provide longer stretches of days off, or they are afraid of being stuck on a fixed shift they dislike, especially if they have low seniority). Only 10 percent of shift workers who work 8-hour shifts would select the straight afternoon shift or

Figure 4-6. Fixed shift preferences.

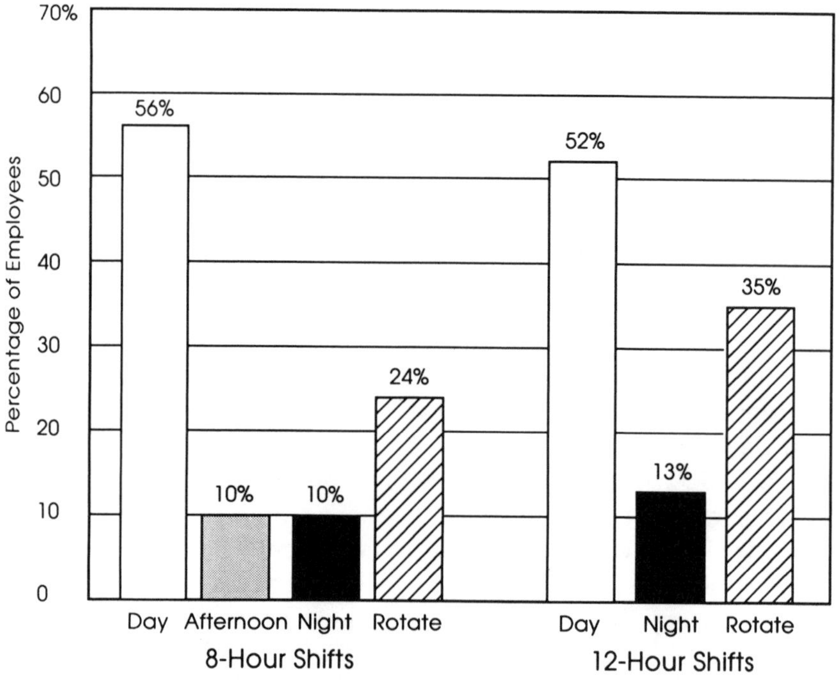

Source: CCG Normative Data Base.

straight night shift as their first choice. On a 24-hour balanced-coverage schedule, 33 percent will get days, 33 percent afternoons, and 33 percent nights. The odds of employees' being stuck on an unpreferred shift go up dramatically in this situation. It's not unusual for half the workforce to be dissatisfied with their schedule. How employees view a fixed schedule depends not only on how their current shift assignment meets their lifestyle but also on their chances of getting onto their preferred shift in the near future. If there is a good possibility of bidding to a preferred shift in the near future, the outlook is positive; if opportunities are limited, increasing numbers of shift workers will become dissatisfied. In the latter scenario, shift workers may quit rather than stay on a shift they don't like—sometimes giving up $10,000 in overtime, shift differential, and holiday pay.

With a 12-hour fixed shift system, the preferences change, since the evening shift no longer exists as an option. Thirty-five percent in this situation would prefer to rotate, and 13 percent would pick straight nights. In a balanced workload 50 percent of the workforce will be on nights. The result is likely to be a large group—about 37 percent—stuck on a shift they don't want, and they'll be really stuck on 12-hour night shifts. With only one other option available, employee morale problems may intensify.

Of course, fixed shifts will be the Best Cost Schedule in some facilities. Many 24-hour businesses have unbalanced workloads. If your unbalanced workload requires only 13 percent of your workforce to work 12-hour night shifts, you could have 100 percent employee schedule satisfaction, since Figure 4-6 indicates that on average, 13 percent preferred a fixed 12-hour night shift. Furthermore, if you are able to offer a variety of staggered starting times, you may also be able to reduce some employee problems with fixed shifts.

Rotating Shifts

For some shift workers, industries, and companies, rotating shifts are accepted as a way of life. The schedules are easily managed and accepted by workers, families, and communities. I have seen communities where religious services are extended to all hours, and I've also seen bars open and fully occupied at 7:00 A.M. after the night shift finishes up. In addition, since everyone rotates through the same schedule of days, afternoons, nights, weekends, and holidays, rotating shifts provide a more equitable experience. Of course, on a poorly designed rotating schedule, everyone will have the same horrific experience, whereas on a good rotating schedule, everyone will reap the same rewards. If the schedules are poorly designed and the rotation pattern is unhealthy, with constantly changing hours and little time off to recuperate, the result will be fatigue, poor performance, and burnout. Rotating schedules may be more disruptive than fixed shifts on family and social life in terms of time off, but it will depend on the schedules. We have encountered companies with rotating schedules that change shifts every 5 days and only have six complete weekends off per year, but we've also seen rotating schedules that provide nearly 40 weekends off a year and rotate quarterly.

Rotating shifts are therefore neither good nor bad; their success will depend on how successfully they meet the needs of each of the three key design circles. Generally employees who are used to rotating shifts will prefer rotating shifts over fixed shifts.

There are thousands of types of rotating shift schedules. The same rotating schedule may look bizarre for one location but normal somewhere else. In Europe, for example, a common and widely accepted model is a rapid rotation requiring employees to work 2 day shifts, have 24 hours off, work 2 afternoon shifts, have 24 hours off, work 2 night shifts, and then have 2 or 3 days off. This schedule is consistently rated low by American shift workers. There are also very slowly rotating schedules, common in wastewater utilities, where rotations may occur every quarter (work 3 months on days, then 3 months on afternoons, and then 3 months on nights). These are also rated low by other American shift workers. American shift workers favor rotating either every week (52.8 percent) or every 2 to 4 weeks (47.2 percent), probably because this is what they are used to.

Extended Workdays

In the 1970s and early 1980s resistance to extended shift systems, primarily 12-hour shifts, was enormous. The modern 40-hour workweek with 12-hour shifts (remember, 12-hour shifts are an old concept from the late 1800s) started in refineries and chemical plants primarily in Canada and were passed down to sister plants in the Gulf Coast area. Initially they were met with resistance by a majority of managers and shift workers, especially in union operations. Now many shift workers and unions have changed their stance.

From the employee viewpoint, the major advantage of extended workdays is the opportunity to increase the number of days off without decreasing pay and benefits. The major negative is there is very little free time remaining in workdays. With getting ready for work, commuting, meals, and sleeping, a 12-hour shift worker is lucky to have an hour or two with his or her family during workdays. Every shift schedule has a conflict between time off and work hours. For example, an 8-hour shift worker who saves up for a long weekend break of 5 days pays the price of working seven consecutive shifts. With a 12-hour shift system, the employee works longer hours and gives up free time on working days in order to double days off.

Shift workers view 12-hour shifts primarily in terms of how they affect their time off and ability to work. For some physically demanding jobs, 12 hours is too long. And individual circumstances matter. Shift workers at a refinery in Minnesota, for example, didn't like 12 hours because it didn't allow them the time they needed every day to manage their dairy farms.

When you're considering a 12-hour shift, your employees need to be told what the actual schedule will be, not just the master. For example, the new master schedule may promise 182 days off per year but the shift workers may be on call for 45 days and actually called in 10 days. In that case, the actual new schedule has the penalty of working long 12-hour shifts, plus unpredictable days off, and the benefits may not be worth it. Prior to implementation, each shift worker can be given an accurate estimate of what actual time off will be.

Although not all shift workers want 12-hour shift systems, there has been a significant growth in employee interest and support for extended shifts (see Figure 4-7). This interest is extending to some of the most unexpected environments. In 1991, I was invited to give a speech to the Coal Miners Union in Australia, a centralized union whose members work 7- and 8-hour shift sched-

Figure 4-7. Percentage of shift workers willing to consider a 12-hour shift system.

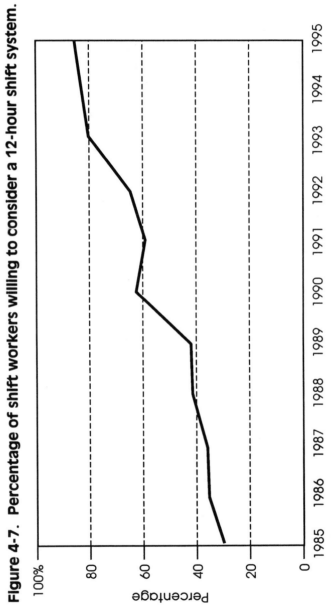

Source: CCG Normative Database.

ules. Since I was a controversial speaker—advocating change and alternative schedules—I was put on the agenda when the meeting was supposed to be over, at 5:00 P.M. When I started my speech, most of the delegates were chatting as they got ready to leave the hall. I put up a 12-hour schedule and said, "It doesn't matter whether you listen or not; your members will be working this type of schedule. Maybe not today, maybe not tomorrow, but it's definitely going to happen." They quieted down and listened. Three years later, several hundred of their union members in Queensland pressured their union leaders to get that schedule at a new site. They did. In Chapter 5, we'll discuss in more detail the pros and cons of 12-hour shift models.

Supervisors and Shift Work

Shift work supervisors wear two caps, managerial and shift worker, which can be a stressful situation. Supervisors are likely to have previously been hourly members of the crew they are supervising, and they work the same around-the-clock schedule as their supervisees, often without overtime pay. They are also supposed to be part of the management team. Shift work supervisors often work the longest hours; they might need to come in early and stay late to provide shift-to-shift turnover, and there may be meetings required with the day management team as well.

The position can be very stressful, but good schedules can make a difference. In many organizations—Tenneco, Pacific Gas & Electric, and British Petroleum, to name a few—shift schedule changes have been developed just to assist the supervisors. In some unionized companies the opposite occurs: The union membership may switch schedules after negotiations with managers, and the supervisors, without any input, are forced to change as well. Even if the hourly workforce is on a different schedule, it is possible to maintain a primary supervisor with corresponding schedules. (In a corresponding schedule system hourly workers are on one schedule and supervisors on another, but each hourly person sees his or her primary supervisor the great majority of work shifts.) Since shift supervisors are often the link between day management and shift work, their schedule should have a built-in sequence where they work the same hours as the core management group.

When you are changing schedules, remember to invite your supervisors to participate. On the other hand, don't let them design the new schedule. They tend to put on their shift work cap in that moment, and you are likely to get a schedule in which the employee circle is given precedence over the business circle. Supervisors' shift preferences are usually similar to those of the people they supervise, and they will be satisfied with the same schedule.

Other Enhancements to the Employee Circle

If you have a shift work schedule that employees just don't like, no amount of education or policy change will fix it. However, if you have a good schedule, you can improve shift work at your facility with some of the following actions:

- Schedule top management, operations management, safety management, training staff, engineering staff, and human resources management to work part of each month on back-shift hours.
- Keep your cafeteria open 24 hours a day with nutritional food, and hire a nutritionist to work with your shift workers and their families. There is no special shift work diet, but basic education and arranging a consistent meal schedule will have a positive impact.
- Keep a gym, or at minimum an exercise station, open around the clock; make it available during breaks, lunches, and before and after shifts.
- Schedule meetings or functions with the shift workers in mind. Let them help determine these times. Don't call shift workers in on their days off. For a rotating shift worker, a Monday meeting at 8:00 A.M. may be equivalent to a manager's coming in on Saturday night at 7:00 P.M. Do not schedule meetings or meals with the night crew in the morning!

Would you want to stay at the plant for a 5:00 P.M. dinner meeting?

- Invite families to the plant. Educate them about the mental and physical stress that shift workers deal with (81 percent report their job as mentally demanding, 60 percent physically demanding). Educate them on your schedule and policies and how they can assist their shift workers.
- Find out which employee concerns the company may be able to help with (e.g., child care, education), and then do something to help.
- Provide 24-hour security at the plant and parking lot and 24-hour access to medical care.
- Provide reasonable policies for sleepy employees, including transportation home after overtime shifts or even after night shifts for employees who are exceptionally sleepy.

The Situation at Renison

Let's check in with Dick Scallan at Renison to see how the employee desires circle was met at their location. I asked him what the scheduling issues were from the employee viewpoint. He told me:

The proof of the pudding in this particular case is that the new schedule allowed people freedom. We ended up having an extra 52 days off each year. Also, the quality of life has improved, and spouses are very, very fond of the new schedule. Some told me they were pretty nervous about "that schedule change" and that they had some misgivings. But now they tell me, "Dick, this is the most fantastic thing we've experienced. We would just like to thank you for that. It has made such a difference in our lifestyle." When people from other mines talk to us about their lifestyle and shift schedules and so on, it's the difference between night and day. Many people in the area wish they could work the schedule we do. Even though we have gone more to a continuous operation, overall employee morale is higher.

With the old 8-hour shifts, people never got to go away, but now with the added time off, lifestyles have changed. People are doing things they have never done before. A lot of people are buying homes up the coast. This is one of the things I was quite keen on: that people have options in their lives and make a choice—stay here or stay at the coast, or whatever they wished. Family life is important. What we didn't have was a sense of community, and now we have that. The underground miners were so pleased; they were really fearful that we'd go for 12-hour shifts. Their biggest concern was that they might have to go to 12-hour shifts, 7 days a week. They had once had a terrible experience with a 12-hour schedule before I got here.

Conclusion

For employees, good shift work schedules can make a shift worker's lifestyle as or more attractive than any day worker's. Bad schedules, on the other hand, can destroy any hope of a reasonable family/social life.

Because of the information explosion, we have found today's shift workers are more aware of the world around them, are more open to change, and are looking at more alternatives than ever before. If you can get past the initial emotional reactions, most are interested in looking at alternate schedule options. In Chapter 5 we will put the three circles together and search for the ultimate schedule.

5

Understanding Schedules

"What's the best schedule?" In 1979, when I began my career as a shift work consultant, I would try to avoid answering this question because I didn't have enough experience with schedules. Fifteen years later, after designing thousands of schedules, I am confident enough to answer, "I don't know what the best schedule is, but I certainly know what a bad one looks like":

• At one refinery on the Gulf Coast, a brilliant engineer had proved he could handle many different tasks, and handle them well. He had assignments in operations, finance, and capital projects, and really understood the workings of the refinery. Then he was asked to design a shift schedule to give employees more weekends off. He came up with an innovative solution: completely different day-off patterns for each of the four crews, using 8- and 12-hour shift lengths. Unfortunately, a key feature of the schedule was that the night shift started at 3:00 A.M.

• A 100-year-old chemical plant had a tradition of allowing any shift worker to design schedules that management would implement if the worker could convince enough other employees to go along. This system was inadvertently encouraged because the schedule would be named after the person who designed it: the Tom Schedule, the Dick Schedule, the Harry Schedule. This was great for the self-esteem of the employees who came up with the ideas. Not surprisingly, this company is still looking for the schedule that meets its business needs.

• A shift schedule at a mining operation took into account all of the latest research findings on health and safety requirements, circadian rhythms, and so on. The schedule was designed to match the body's rotations so start times were gradually delayed during rotation by 2 to 3 hours. It was one of the healthiest schedules ever dreamed up. Of course, the shift workers, their families, their supervisors—no one—could ever plan anything in advance because the start times kept changing. Carpools were impossible. It was a disaster for everyone and was quickly thrown out. It was the first schedule I ever helped design and implement.

If you're reading this chapter to find "the answer," the single schedule that will solve every shift work problem for every business, you will be disappointed. There is no single best schedule that fits every situation. But if you want to learn how to classify any schedule and evaluate its impact on your business, the first part of this chapter should be beneficial. The second part of this chapter reviews some key scheduling issues to help you in your schedule design. If you spend appropriate effort on determining your needs, you will find several suitable schedules.

Part I: Classification and Analysis of the Schedule

In shift work consulting, one of the basic rules is, "You can never understand the current schedule well enough." However, shift workers, first-line supervisors, and facility managers frequently cannot fully describe their shift schedule. Shift workers will describe their schedule by the shift: "I'm working evenings." The line supervisors will tell you, "We have a three-shift schedule." The plant manager says, "We run 5 days a week." They are all right, and they are all wrong.

To understand and compare shift schedules, it is critical to have a classification system, so everyone is speaking the same language. A classification system helps you to understand the assumptions behind your current schedule and to cost out and compare alternative models. Let's look at a manufacturing company whose schedule runs Monday through Friday, with Saturday and Sunday off, with 8-hour day, evening, and night shifts, each equally staffed. Coleman Consulting Group classifies this as a 120-40, balanced, 3-crew, 8-hour, fixed, 5-2. How do we arrive at this? Let's look further at the schedule in the next pages and at Figure 5-1.

How to Classify Schedules

To classify, first look vertically at the schedule, like an operations manager, to understand the coverage. In Figure 5-1, the first group of employees to report is the night crew, who start the week at 11:00 P.M. Sunday night and finish at 7:00 A.M. Monday morning. Since this crew starts the workweek for the entire plant, it is Crew 1. Looking down the schedule, we see that the next crew to come in is the day crew, or Crew 2, covering from 7:00 A.M. to 3:00 P.M. At 3:00 P.M. on Monday, Crew 3 takes over and works the afternoon shift until 11:00 P.M. Monday. Twenty-four hours of coverage is completed.

The *n* on Tuesday means that Crew 1 will report to work at 11:00 P.M. on Monday night to maintain coverage until they are off at 7:00 A.M. Tuesday (8 hours). If you continue to look down the schedule, you'll see that Crew 3 closes out the workweek on Friday at 11:00 P.M. Then the operation closes down until next week, Sunday at 11:00 P.M., when Crew 1 starts up again. The cycle repeats

Figure 5-1. Schedule example (120–40, balanced, 3-crew, 8-hour, fixed, 5-2).

Crew	M	T	W	T	F	S	S
1	n	n	n	n	n	–	–
2	d	d	d	d	d	–	–
3	a	a	a	a	a	–	–

n = nights   = 11 P.M.–7 A.M. (first shift of the work week; starts at 11 P.M. Sunday)
d = days   = 7 A.M.–3 P.M.
a = afternoons = 3 P.M.–11 P.M.
– = off

each week. Figure 5-1 is a snapshot of the coverage for 1 week. There are 24 hours of coverage occurring 5 days a week, for a total of 120 operating hours. So this schedule is called a "120."

Shift workers view schedules from a completely different perspective. They look *across* the schedule, and mainly at the dashes, or day-off pattern. For example, if you are on Crew 3, the afternoon crew, you start each shift at 3:00 P.M. and get off at 11:00 P.M. Your workweek is Monday through Friday, and your prime time off stretches from 11:00 P.M. Friday until 3:00 P.M. Monday. The pattern is repeated every week. Shift workers also view the schedule financially. Because of possible overtime, the dash on Saturday may be viewed as a potential time-and-a-half shift and Sunday as potential double time.

Because the average workweek in this master schedule is 40 hours, the schedule is called a 120-40 (for 120 total operating hours for the entire plant and 40 hours for each employee). If the employees had a schedule wherein one week they work 36 hours and the next week they work 44 hours, which is common in many shift schedules, it would still be a 120-40, because the average workweek is 40 hours. (In Chapter 6, we will see how even in a schedule with 36- and 44-hour workweeks, no extra overtime costs are accrued if implemented properly.)

The next critical variable in any schedule is whether the staffing is balanced or unbalanced; in other words, are the same number of employees scheduled at all hours? Assume we have fifty employees on each of the three crews. Now, we would have a 120-40 balanced. We would have unbalanced coverage if there were sixty employees on day shift, thirty employees on afternoon shift, and ten on night shift. (This unbalanced coverage would not total 120 full operating hours but would be equivalent to 67 full hours.)

The next important variable is the number of crews. As described in Chapter 2, a crew is a group of people following the same day-off pattern and/or work hours. There are three crews in our sample schedule, so this is a 120-40, balanced, 3-crew. (It's also possible to cover 120 hours with two crews, four crews, seven crews, eight crews, or other combination.) The number of crews will have a significant impact on cross training, flexibility, skill balance, supervision, communication, and teamwork.

Length of shift is the next variable to consider. In our example

8 hours is the choice, but we have implemented shifts with lengths from 4 to 12.5 hours. Later in this chapter we will discuss shift length options in detail.

The next issue to consider is shift structure. There are six basic types:

1. *Fixed Shifts* (also called straight shifts): Each crew has its own set hours, which are permanent and do not change— for example, three 8-hour shifts (11:00 P.M.–7:00 A.M., 7:00 A.M.–3:00 P.M., 3:00 P.M.–11:00 P.M.) or two 12-hour shifts (6:00 A.M.–6:00 P.M. and 6:00 P.M.–6:00 A.M.).
2. *Rotating Shifts:* Each crew works an equal sequence of days, afternoons, and nights, regularly changing to the next set.
3. *Oscillating Shifts:* One group of shift workers is on fixed shifts and the remaining groups rotate.
4. *Primary Shifts:* Each crew has a fixed shift but occasionally works the opposite shift.
5. *Staggered Shifts:* These are fixed shifts with numerous start times and numerous crews.
6. *Mixed Shifts:* A combination of two or more of these systems is worked in the same department.

The last variable to consider is days off. Are they fixed or rotating? Is the same pattern followed for each crew or different? What is the pattern? In our example, the days off are the same for each crew, fixed, Saturday and Sunday, and the pattern is 5 days on and 2 days off, or a "5-2." If the days off are rotating, some description of the pattern (e.g., 6 on, 2 off) is stated. With a 6-2, days off are always changing (Monday and Tuesday one week, Tuesday and Wednesday the next week, and so on).

Many shift systems are classified solely by the day-off pattern, a mistake that can cost millions of dollars. We have seen corporations with excess capital equipment of $400 million because their capital decisions were made on a limited 5-day schedule with weekends off. The current schedule for most 24-hour businesses is not based on an engineered, deliberate selection process but often developed for historical reasons that no longer apply ("That's the way we've always done it"). It's rare for anyone at the site to know who actually designed the schedule, and the key operating assumption behind the design may have long been forgotten. Schedules are just accepted. Ask yourself who designed the schedule at your facility, and whether it is cost-effective.

Analyzing the Schedule

To review the positives and negatives of this 120-40 schedule system, let's say you own a manufacturing plant that has been in business for about 20 years. Every few years, you have purchased new capital equipment because your sales are steadily increasing. To analyze your schedule, it's helpful to review the three key schedule design dimensions one at a time.

The Business View

From the business viewpoint, the major advantages of the schedule are that there is no built-in overtime, the staffing ratio is low (it requires hiring only three employees to cover one 24-hour position), and downtime is built in on the weekend, which may allow opportunities (albeit expensive overtime) to catch up on customer orders, maintenance, and product changes.

On the negative side, capital utilization is low and may cost the plant millions of dollars in extra equipment or lost opportunities. (Remember, there are 8,760 hours in a year. Shutting down for weekends, holidays, summer shutdown, lunch and breaks, and with equipment up time of 85 percent, utilization is probably below 50 percent.) Over the years management has probably bought new capital equipment rather than fully utilizing equipment on hand. In addition, costs associated with starting up and shutting down equipment every week may be expensive in terms of wasted material, wasted labor, poor yield, and quality. Maintenance scheduling is likely to be inefficient and expensive. Overtime may be very high. Communication, lack of training, skill imbalance, and employee turnover on some shifts are likely problems. If we added up all the costs, your "simple" schedule may be costing your business several million dollars a year, enough to turn a loss into a profit.

Be skeptical when you see a schedule like this. For example, when I saw a schedule operating 120 hours per week at a beverage manufacturer, my first comment to management was: "Aren't you lucky that your customers' total demand (thirst) for juice across the United States adds up to exactly 120 hours run-time a week." It just so happens that if management hired three crews, each would have a 40-hour workweek without overtime. How come your customers' demand doesn't require you to produce 118.3 hours, or 147.1 hours, or 92 hours, or 155 hours? Or maybe the operating hours per week should vary by season. The 120-40 schedule is quite arbitrary. The odds that it is the right schedule for a business are 1 in 168! (There are 168 hours in a week.) Determining the correct number of operating hours is the first important calculation in selecting a schedule for your business.

Health and Safety Requirements

From the health and safety perspective, the schedule affects each crew differently. The day crew's circadian rhythms (Factor I) are in sync, and sleep debt (Factor II) is minimal; they work 5 days in a row, followed by 2 days off to recuperate. However, if weekend overtime is scheduled, they will work 12 consecutive days and likely build up a significant sleep debt.

The afternoon crew may have enhanced circadian adjustment if they keep the same late sleep time and wakeup time 7 days a week, on days off as well as days worked. Other afternoon employees will get off work at 11:00 P.M., fall asleep at 2:00 A.M., and then need to be up at 6:00 A.M. or 7:00 A.M. to help their family start their day. This lifestyle doesn't mesh with the schedule and will promote the buildup of sleep debt.

The night crew invariably has a circadian rhythm problem because their bodies spend the equivalent of 5 days a week in the United States, followed by 2 days in a country halfway around the world. Decreased alertness at work could be a problem. The overall health, performance, and safety impact of this schedule will be heavily determined by whether there is balanced staffing. The lower the percentage of the workforce scheduled for nights, the better will be the overall health and safety rating.

Employee Desires

How the schedule rates from the employee viewpoint depends on your shift preference and overtime situation. If you are a day shift employee and that's your preferred shift, and right now overtime is low and you prefer time off over overtime, it's a great schedule. If you are on the night shift and that's your least preferred shift, and you depend on overtime and there isn't any, the schedule could be disastrous. Depending on each employee's family, social life, and financial needs, the schedule will be rated accordingly. Nevertheless, there is some common ground. Almost all employees would agree that scheduled weekends off and working only 5 days in a row is a major benefit.

What are the odds of everyone getting a preferred shift? From our normative database (see Chapter 4), we know that for 8-hour fixed shifts, 56 percent of shift workers prefer days, 10 percent prefer afternoons, and 10 percent prefer nights, while 24 percent prefer rotating shifts. In our plant with the balanced staffing scenario we would expect 53 percent satisfied and 47 percent dissatisfied with their shift placement.

Every schedule issue can be evaluated using this three-circle approach. Let's try to determine the best starting time for 12-hour shifts. From a business viewpoint, noon and midnight are advantageous because the daytime managers working 8:00 A.M. to 4:00 P.M. will be able to see both shifts every day for at least 4 hours. U.S. shift workers prefer 6:00 A.M. to 6:00 P.M. (24 percent), 7:00 A.M. to 7:00 P.M. (23 percent), and 5:00 A.M. to 5:00 P.M. (17 percent). These choices are motivated primarily by the desire to get the best commute times and family mealtime. From the health and safety circle, shifts should end while it's still dark outside so the night shift can get into bed without exposure to sunlight. The start time should change in the different seasons—maybe 4:30 A.M. in summer and 6:30 A.M. in winter. Weighing and balancing the three circles for your facility will yield your best answer.

Models Versus Schedules

To understand the wide range of schedule options, it's helpful to make a distinction between a model and a schedule. A *model* is a system for deploying capital and personnel with a key operations concept and numerous derived schedules. A *schedule* is one of a number of day-off patterns derived from a model with employee buy-in and work, pay, and coverage policies tailored to that schedule. Some models have only 10 to 20 derived schedules; other models have over 1,000 derived schedules. For example, before 1980 one of the most common models in continuous operations was a weekly rotating schedule with 7-day work blocks nicknamed the Southern Swing. (Actually, we classify it as a 168-42, balanced, 4-crew, 8-hour, weekly rotating, 28-day cycle model.) The key concept in its design is balanced 7-day coverage with 5 percent built-in overtime. We have identified over 1,000 variations (schedules) of that one model that meet all of the criteria. The variations include different day-off patterns, different positions of the long breaks, different start day of the week, different rotation cycles, and others. Yet all the derived schedules share the same basic features so that most managers will recognize it as the same model. Figure 5-2 lists six of the thousand possibilities. Below is a listing of the design advantage of each:

1. *128-Hour Long Break:* Longest possible weekend off for employees without excessive overtime costs.
2. *Double Sunday:* Where a maintenance shift is needed and/or employees are given flexibility for overtime or many employees observe Sunday as a religious day.
3. *96-Hour Transition:* Emphasis on health and safety, allowing three equal 96-hour breaks to assist rotation.
4. *Shift Breaker:* Only 40-hour workweeks are allowed and a few day shift positions are made available for highly crossed-trained, senior employees.
5. *Clockwise 120-Hour-Long Change:* Longest possible weekend (without excessive overtime costs) with healthier direction of rotation.
6. *Sunday Premium Pay:* When Sunday is a double-time day, the day-off pattern can allow 3 days off in 1 week without costing the company extra money. In this case the long break is Friday, Saturday, Sunday, Monday, and Tuesday.

Analysis of the Southern Swing Schedule

To make sure you understand how to analyze schedules, here's one more example. From a business perspective, the South-

Figure 5-2. Southern Swing model (168–42, balanced, 4-crew, 8-hour, weekly rotating, 28-day-off cycle) and six derived schedules.

Models vs. Schedules
Model

Week/Crew	1	2	3	4	5	6	7
1	d	d	d	d	d	d	d
2	a	a	a	a	a	a	a
3	n	n	n	n	n	n	n
4	-	-	-	-	-	-	-

d = days   a = afternoons   n = nights   – = off

This model has over 1,000 derived schedules. For example:

① **128-Hour Long Break**

Week/Crew	M	T	W	T	F	S	S
1	n	n	n	n	n	-	-
2	-	-	a	a	a	a	a
3	a	a	-	d	d	d	d
4	d	d	d	-	-	n	n

n = 1st

④ **Shift Breaker**

Week/Crew	S	M	T	W	T	F	S
1	d	d*	d*	d*	d*	d*	-
2	-	-	a	a	a	a	a
3	a	a	-	-	n	n	n
4	n	n	n	n	-	-	d

n = 1st * = shift breaker coverage options

② **Double Sunday**

Week/Crew	S	S	M	T	W	T	F
1	d	d	d	d	d	-	-
2	-	-	a	a	a	a	a
3	a	*	-	-	n	n	n
4	n	n	n	-	-	d	d

d = 1st * = double, split shift, voluntary or mandatory overtime

⑤ **Clockwise—120-Hour Long Change**

Week/Crew	M	T	W	T	F	S	S
1	n	n	n	n	n	-	-
2	-	-	d	d	d	d	d
3	d	d	-	-	a	a	a
4	a	a	a	a	-	n	n

d = 1st

③ **96-Hour Transitions**

Week/Crew	M	T	W	T	F	S	S
1	d	d	d	d	d	-	-
2	-	a	a	a	a	a	a
3	a	-	-	n	n	n	n
4	n	n	n	-	-	d	d

d = 1st

⑥ **Sunday Premium Pay**

Week/Crew	M	T	W	T	F	S	S
1	a	a	a	a	-	-	-
2	-	-	n	n	n	n	n
3	n	n	-	d	d	d	d
4	d	d	d	-	a	a	a

n = 1st

ern Swing model has full capital utilization but does not cover discretionary workload. Training and value-added activities will be schedule busters, and communication is difficult. The model may be expensive because it uses built-in overtime to cover core workload. This model tends to promote a crew concept, not a team concept.

From a health and safety viewpoint, the model falls short on both Factor I (circadian adjustment) and Factor II (sleep debt). Employees are forced to rotate weekly and in some schedules, to earlier hours (or eastbound), the more difficult direction. Just when there's a chance to adjust to new hours, it's time to rotate. Sleep debt and fatigue can build up from the long stretches of consecutive workdays. In some schedules, these two factors converge when a difficult rotation occurs in the middle of working 14 of 15 days. Any additional overtime on this schedule will result in more fatigue. Safety and alertness is problematic, and operation errors may be costly. This is the type of model that was worked during the incidents at Three Mile Island and the nuclear power plant shut down by the NRC.

This model looks unattractive from the employee perspective (working 7 days in a row, with only 13 weekends off per year), but it usually has a good number of supporters because of the "survivor factor." Many shift workers who cannot tolerate this model have already dropped out of shift work so a senior shift work "survivor group," with a strong influence in squashing any attempts at change, may remain. Nevertheless, this schedule, which was one of the most common in continuous industries 30 years ago, is becoming rarer and should be nearly extinct in another decade.

To summarize, a schedule that on the surface appears to meet the basic business needs by covering 168 hours may not be the Best Cost Schedule. Be wary of the management slogan, "We don't care what schedule employees work, as long as the new one doesn't cost us more (in labor costs)." The hidden costs of a poor schedule can have a multimillion-dollar impact on your bottom line.

When working with employees to implement a new schedule, it's much better to start out with models. It is easier to work together to determine the schedule (day-off pattern, work, pay, coverage rules) later. If you try to select the schedule first, you may have tremendous problems reaching a consensus.

In our consulting work we have developed hundreds of major schedule models, each with a key operating principle. The key concepts behind models vary considerably. For example, the 120-40, balanced, 3-crew, 8-hour, fixed, Monday through Friday model has the key concept of "maintain a 40-hour workweek and day shift mentality." More advanced models have more advanced key concepts. The concept for the 168-40, unbalanced, 5-crew, 12- and 8-hour combination day-off pattern is, "reliable employee coverage will be rewarded with better time off." The key concept in the 168-41.3, unbalanced, 3-crew, 8- and 12-hour fixed model is, "improve skill balance within a fixed shift system." This is achieved by making the usually least attractive shift the most attractive.

Master Schedule Versus Actual Schedule

When classifying schedules, remember to distinguish between the master schedule, the one described in the employee handbook or posted once a year on a bulletin board or schedule card, and the actual schedule, the one really used and traditionally managed by first-line supervision on a daily basis. The actual schedule includes overtime, vacations, sickness, product changes, shutdown, downtime, maintenance, and so forth. It's not unusual for the actual schedule to be very different from the master schedule. For example, at a power plant near Evansville, Indiana, the master schedule had shift workers working five 8-hour shifts with 2 days off each week. In practice, due to a cluster of early retirements and a hiring freeze, shift workers were actually working six consecutive 12-hour shifts with 1 day off each week.

A classic example of a gap between the master and actual schedule is a 120-40 being worked as a 168-56. Employees, normally scheduled to be off 2 days per week, are forced in on Saturday and Sunday to cover an unusually high workload. This solution is expensive, unsafe, and poor for morale, especially if it stays in place for several months. If this type of high workload is steady and predictable, consider a different schedule. One manufacturer in Missouri had a 120-40 master schedule but for 10 consecutive years worked full crews on Saturdays; thus, the actual schedule was a 144-48. A 144-40 (a 6-day schedule without overtime) would have been less costly for such a predictable workload.

Remember, not only can you design any number of weekly operating hours but you can also select any average workweek you require; separate the operating schedule from the employee schedule when contemplating your design.

Current Modified Models

When considering alternate schedules, you might want to consider a current modified model, which has the important key concept that no big changes are needed (or from the employees' perspective, "Every time something changes around here, things get worse, but I'm willing to risk tweaking our schedule just a little"). One of many possible current modified schedules for the 120-40 we've been discussing is shown in Figure 5-3.

At first glance this schedule looks exactly like the schedule shown in Figure 5-1. It should, because "current modified" means "a small change." Operations now start each week at 3:00 P.M. Sunday with Crew 3 and finish at 3:00 P.M. Friday afternoon with Crew 2 (remember to look vertically). In this model, Crew 3 (which is working 3:00 P.M. to 11:00 P.M., or the afternoon shift) now starts its workweek on Sunday at 3:00 P.M. and finishes the workweek on Thursday at 11:00 P.M. (remember to read across).

From the business viewpoint, the impact of this schedule is negligible. There may be a slight savings in utility costs because

Figure 5-3. Current modified model (120–40, balanced, 3-crew, 8-hour, fixed, 5-2).

Crew	M	T	W	T	F	S	S
1	n	n	n	n	n	–	–
2	d	d	d	d	d	–	–
3	a	a	a	a	–	–	a

n = nights = 11 P.M.–7 A.M. (first shift of the work week; starts at 3 P.M. Sunday)
d = days = 7 A.M.–3 P.M.
a = afternoons = 3 P.M.–11 P.M.
– = off

the plant will have transferred 8 hours of weekday operations to a weekend, or an increase in expenses if you offer Sunday premium instead of following federal overtime laws. In the health and safety circle, there is no change, since the employees are still working 5 days on, 2 days off, fixed shifts. In the employee circle, there may be a slight improvement. Often employees with the least seniority end up on the afternoon shift. Because they usually are young and single, they may also enjoy maintaining late hours and sleeping in. They might prefer to have Friday and Saturday nights off, prime hours for socializing. Sunday afternoon (traditionally a family time) may not be as important to them.

Is everyone going to like this modification? Of course not. Does it have a major impact on your business or improve profitability? No. Do not expect a current modified to have a great impact—it's a small change that usually affects only one of the three key schedule design circles. (In our example we made a small change in the employee circle. It is possible to have a current modified that affects any circle.) However, if you are trying to make just a minor improvement, a current modified could be your solution.

Part II: Schedule Design Issues

Now that we have finished our classification and analysis system, let's discuss some common schedule design issues. It's impossible to cover all topics, so I have selected those that should cover most readers' interest: fixed shifts, rotating shifts, shift lengths, weekend warrior models, and fly in/fly out operations.

Fixed Shifts

Fixed shifts, characterized by groups of employees always working the same hours, can be used in 3-, 4-, 5-, 6-, or 7-day-per-week operations. Although the most common fixed schedule design for 24-hour coverage is the 120-40, 3-crew, 8-hour, 5-2 discussed earlier, we frequently recommend fixed shift systems with as few as two crews and up to eight crews. In Australia a 76-38, 2-crew, 8-hour, fixed shift with a 9-day fortnight day-off pattern is common in manufacturing, and a 120-35, 4-crew, 7-hour, fixed shift, 5-2 is common in underground coal mines in New South Wales.

As a general rule, fixed shifts are advantageous when the workload is unbalanced. If a 24-hour business with 100 employees requires 50 percent staffing during daylight hours, 30 percent during afternoon hours, and 20 percent during night hours, it is simple to allocate 50 employees to the day crew, 30 to afternoons, and 20 for nights. Rotating shifts can also be used to cover this workload, but they are more complicated to manage. Departments such as laboratories, maintenance, and support services, or service industries where 24-hour coverage is needed but the workload is mainly geared toward days, are most appropriate for fixed shifts.

Otherwise fixed shifts may not be advantageous from the business perspective. Businesses that know from the outset they have balanced workloads requiring 8,760 hours per year coverage (utilities, steel mills, refineries) almost always choose rotating shift systems to avoid the problem of skill imbalance frequently associated with fixed shifts. If skill imbalance in rotating shifts is costly to the operation, reassigning employees to another crew with minimal disruption is simple.

Many of the problems of fixed shifts can be overcome with a few critical policy changes. If your fixed shift system is costing you money, you don't have to go to rotating shifts to fix it. For example, if management has the right to place an individual on any shift, skill balance could be achieved, even with fixed shifts. This solution, however, goes against the seniority system, which is prevalent in many industries. Therefore, another solution is that first employees must be qualified in order to exercise their shift bid preference, then honor seniority.

If communication is a problem on fixed shifts, schedule management to work occasional night shifts with flexible schedules. Instead of first making the dramatic move from fixed to rotating shifts, consider whether oscillating or primary shifts are applicable. Perhaps an innovative schedule that makes one of the back shifts more attractive than day shift would be another solution. (For example, the night shift gets most of the weekends off.)

There are many schedule models for running 7 days a week with fixed shifts. The 168-56, 3-crew, 8-hour, discussed earlier (where three Monday through Friday crews work weekend overtime) is inappropriate except for short-term workload increases; it's expensive for management, eliminates employee time off, and pushes the limits of health and safety. By adding personnel to each of the three fixed crews, the schedule can be adjusted to a 168-40. Then the business can run every hour, without overtime, and employees can be scheduled to work 4, 5, or 6 days a week.

Another frequent but ill-advised solution is to have three fixed crews and add a fourth, rotating crew (often called a *knockout* or *jackrabbit crew*). This special crew usually works a rapid rotation cycle of 2 day shifts, 2 afternoon shifts, 2 night shifts, and 1 day off, filling in for the days off of the other three crews. Most American workers do not view this as an attractive option.

Seven-day fixed shift schedules frequently utilize 12-hour shifts as well. One common model is called a "4-3" (see Figure 5-4). These schedules require 50 percent of the workforce to be on permanent night shifts compared to 33 percent on fixed 8-hour shifts. Worldwide, only 10 percent of employees prefer a fixed, 12-hour night shift. This model has approximately twenty-five viable derived schedules, with the key variations being the length and placement of the swing day.

Figure 5-4. A 7-day fixed shift schedule utilizing 12-hour shifts (168–42, balanced, 4-crew, 12-hour, fixed shifts/ fixed days off with a 4-3/3-4 day-off pattern).

Crew	S	M	T	W	T	F	S
A	D	D	D	*	–	–	–
B	–	–	–	*	D	D	D
C	–	–	–	N	N	N	*
D	N	N	N	–	–	–	*

D = 7 A.M.–7 P.M. (first shift of the week)
N = 7 P.M.–7 A.M.
– = day off
* = alternating day off

Rotating Shifts

Rotating shifts offer several advantages from the business view-point. Since everyone will rotate through the same schedule of days, afternoons, nights, weekends, and holidays, management can place the employees it wants on any crew, thus increasing its chance of having the right skills, at the right place, at the right time. Since all employees rotate through the day shift, interaction between day staff and shift workers is generally better. Of course, rotating schedules have their own problems. If the schedules are poorly designed (constantly changing schedules with little time off to recuperate), they can result in fatigue, poor performance, and safety problems. From the employee viewpoint, rotating shifts may be more disruptive than fixed shifts, depending on social require-ments and family support of the schedule.

Rotating shifts are therefore neither "good" nor "bad" (same as fixed shifts), and their success will depend on how well the exact schedule selected meets the needs of each of the three design cir-cles. Generally employees who are used to rotating shifts will pre-fer them over fixed shifts.

There are hundreds of rotating shift systems. One system may look bizarre for one location but be normal somewhere else. As mentioned previously, in Europe a common and widely accepted schedule is a rapid rotation requiring employees to work 2 day shifts, then have 24 hours off, work 2 afternoon shifts, then have 24 hours off, work 2 night shifts, and then have 2 or 3 days off. In the United States weekly rotation is very common (work 7 days, have 2 off, work 7 afternoons, have 2 off, and then work 7 nights and have 3 off). Rotating schedules with 12-hour shifts have become much more common over the past decade as well.

Rotating and fixed shifts are only two of the six major shift systems (oscillating, primary, staggered, and mixed are the others). Differ-ent situations require different approaches. At Upjohn, fixed shifts were a tradition, but exposure to new technology was considered an important scheduling goal. Here, primary shifts seemed the best answer. At SEH America, the change from a 5-day to 7-day-per week operation was such a major cultural change that management elected to allow a mixed system, putting both rotating and fixed shifts in the same department. The results were that 97 percent of the employees received either their first or second shift preference.

Shift Lengths

Many shift workers and managers care more about shift length than other schedule issues. Companies that have no idea if their current schedule is costing them millions of dollars in lost profits will have a strong position on 12-hour shifts.

There is no best shift length. At Brockway Glass in Oakland, California, one of the jobs required shift workers to identify "stones," or tiny cracks in bottles. Employees sit close to the manufacturing line, bottles whizzing past at tremendous speed and a bright light shining across into their eyes. This task was so arduous that every 15 minutes a new person rotated into the position. We found over half the workforce reported extensive sleepiness during their 15-minute shift. In California, some firefighters work 36-hour shifts and sleep on the job (not, of course, while fighting fires). In this way they are available to respond to emergencies. Clearly a 36-hour shift can be safe.

The right length for shifts will depend on the type of work being performed and the work environment. As a general rule, longer shifts work better when the shift workers are responding to alarms and/or monitoring automated systems. Shorter shifts are compatible with physically demanding work or repetitive motion.

Because we operate on a 24-hour day, shift lengths that are easily divided into 24 generally are easiest to manage and most practical. Hence, three 8-hour shifts or two 12-hour shifts are the most common in 24-hour businesses. Six-hour shifts are another possibility but are rarely used because they require a very high staffing level. With a little effort, other combinations are possible as well. For example, from a health and alertness perspective, night shifts could be 5 hours long while afternoon and day shifts might be 9 or 10 hours.

9- and 10-Hour Shifts

Ten-hour shifts are often seen as a possible solution for jobs where 12-hour shifts might be a little too long but 8-hour shifts can be tolerated fairly easily. Ten-hour shifts require creative schedule design if you want to run 24 hours a day without downtime or overstaffing. If your business requires daily downtime of about 4 hours, then two 10-hour shifts are a good fit. For example, if Crew 1 is working a 10-hour shift from 5:00 A.M. to 3:00 P.M., and Crew 2 is working a 10-hour shift from 3:00 P.M. to 1:00 A.M., there will be 4 hours, from 1:00 A.M. to 5:00 A.M., for maintenance, cleanup, sanitation, blasting, transportation, or a whole host of other downtime activities. There are hundreds of 10-hour shift schedules available ranging from operating 40 hours per week up to 168. However, if your downtime needs to be 1 hour, 3 hours, or 8 hours, or none at all, then 10-hour shifts will be a high-cost schedule.

Don't confuse shift lengths, "10s" or "four 10s," with a complete schedule system. It's not unusual for employees to ask management for four 10s (work Monday through Thursday, 10 hours a day). From the employee perspective, that means the same pay and benefits (or sometimes more pay, because they are working overtime) and 3 days off per week (one weekday in addition to the weekend). Four 10s are frequently implemented, with little thought to their impact on the business. You may end up getting four 8s with 2 extra hours of coffee breaks per day. We have seen numerous businesses go to four 10s, only to find a tremendous decrease in productivity per hour. Other facilities are successful because productivity is measured closely and four 10-hour shifts can reduce set-up times from 5 to 4 hours per week—a 20 percent improvement.

It's hard to go back to five 8s after implementing four 10s, though, because you'll face a drop in morale. (Try taking away fifty-two 3-day weekends!) A utility in Arizona put some of its day workers on four 10s, to reduce employee commutes (1 hour each way) and improve morale. It soon found out that on Fridays and Mondays not enough employees were present to get the work done, and productivity suffered. Asking the employees to increase their commute by 20 percent was not an option, so the organization is trying to make the best of the situation.

Many managers assume all 10-hour shift schedules are the same, but they are not. Homestake Gold Mines in Lead, South Dakota, initially had a poor experience with 10s. To improve productivity and maintain jobs, management won a special concession from the union (Steel Workers) to put in a 10-hour shift without overtime after 8 hours. However, the wrong 10-hour shift schedule was implemented. The schedule was unbalanced even though the workload was balanced. As a result, there were some shifts with too many employees and not enough equipment and other shifts with too much equipment and not enough people. Productivity (tons per man-hour) decreased. After we designed a balanced 10-hour roster (140-40, balanced, 2-crew, 10-hour, fixed), productivity improved 16 percent.

Ulan Coal Mine in New South Wales, Australia, had a similar experience with 9-hour shifts. At Ulan the new schedule gave employees more money and time off but was also supposed to improve productivity. This schedule didn't match the workload efficiently, and production cost per ton went up instead of down, as they had expected. Managers were frustrated, and they wanted to go back to their old 8-hour roster. It took a lot of convincing by our consulting team to get management to realize the excellent opportunity facing them if they implemented the correct 9-hour roster. The union was allowing flexible rostering; management had simply picked the wrong one. Eventually a more productive 9-hour roster (120-35, unbalanced, 3-crew, fixed shift) was implemented. Volunteer overtime on the weekends allowed for the mine to keep up with support tasks such as construction and for overtime hogs to make some extra money. Overall productivity increased by more than 10 percent.

12-Hour Shifts

Before around-the-clock light became available, most large manufacturing plants had only one crew of employees. They averaged an 11-hour workday during the winter and, as daylight hours expanded, up to a 14-hour day during the summer. It was natural for managers in the new capital-intensive "never-put-out-the-fire" industries, such as iron foundries and steel mills, to start out working employees on 12-hour shifts. In 1883, the master schedule required employees to work 12-hour shifts, 27 out of 28 days including one 24-hour shift, and an average 84-hour workweek. This 168-84 was a brutal schedule associated with dramatic safety problems, high death rates in plants, bitter labor management disputes, alcoholism, and family-social problems. The problem was not the 12-hour shifts but the 84-hour workweek.

Today there are hundreds of 12-hour shift systems worked all over the world. Many unions that previously fought for 8-hour days are now considering 12-hour shifts in a new light. I asked Jim Cox, president of Local 125 for the International Brotherhood of Electrical Workers in Portland, Oregon, for his union's perspective on longer shifts:

> I think you have to go back a little bit in history here. Some of our folks were on probably the best 8-hour schedule you can be on, from my perspective. I worked shift work for 12 years, and so I thought they rotated the right way and had the right number of days off—as best as you could do. From the perspective of the union in general, it wasn't until maybe the last five years that our international would even allow us to consider alternative schedules. Their basis was that we had fought for 8-hour days for years, so why should we go back to 10s or 12s? The only way that we were able to work anything but an 8-hour schedule was to do it through a memorandum of agreement on the side, and you didn't let the international even know you had done it. The international finally changed leadership, and the new leadership said, "The issue isn't that we are working 84 or 60 hours a week but that we are still working 40. It's about time we started listening to our membership." So at that point we started openly considering the 12-hour schedules. It's more what the folks want to do.

Since 1984, our consultants have worked with unions in North America, South America, Europe, Africa, the Pacific Rim, and Australia that have supported their members' desire to work 12-hour shifts as long as the average workweek of 35 to 48 hours (depending on the norms for that country) is maintained.

The 12-hour shift is not a schedule model but a variable in schedule design. Twelve-hour shifts can be worked with 40, 60, 80, 100, 120, 160, or any other number of operating hours. The average number of employee work hours per week can be 35, 37.5, 40, 42,

48, 56—again, any option. Most businesses consider a 12-hour schedule only if they're operating 168 hours per week, but if 12s are an advantage when running 7 days a week, why not use them in operations running fewer than 7 days a week? Twelve-hour shifts have been very productive and well received by employees in some locations but have failed miserably in others. There is no blanket rule that 12s are good or bad. However, if a 12-hour model does fit your business needs and there is a commitment to make 12-hour shifts work, it can be done successfully in most businesses.

Twelve-hour shift schedules designed and implemented properly can be a Best Cost Schedule. Since there are more than 1,000 variations, make sure you select one appropriate to your situation. Some 12-hour schedules provide 8-day "long breaks"; others limit the number of consecutive night shifts to one or build in regular training cycles. Some coordinate operators and maintain scheduling, others make it a nightmare. Many industries are finding that their shift workers (occasionally managers) want to try 12-hour shifts to improve time off and productivity, and it's not unusual for a facility to grasp the first 12-hour schedule that comes along. Once a company goes onto a 12-hour schedule, it is nearly impossible to go back to the old 8-hour schedule. Since 12-hour shifts are normally so well liked (81 percent employee support it after a 6- to 12-month trial), it's very hard to make yet another schedule change, so try to build your business needs into the design from the start.

Many shift workers are surprised to learn that working a few 12-hour shifts followed by several days off is healthier than working seven consecutive 8-hour shifts with only 1 or 2 days off. Building in rest breaks and job rotation, educating employees about coping strategies, and developing rational policies for sleepiness on the job are critical elements to a successful 12-hour schedule.

Safety also must be emphasized. Companies such as Du Pont, with up to 20 years of experience in 12-hour shifts, have reported excellent safety records, especially when these schedules are implemented with ongoing safety programs. AMAX Coal won the Sentinel of Safety Award (for the safest surface mine in the United States) in the first year after it implemented a 12-hour schedule that featured a weekly 60-minute safety meeting, continuous communication between drivers, and strategic rest breaks.

If you're implementing a 12-hour shift schedule, be sure to do the following prior to implementation:

- Check viability for each job (e.g.: Is it too physically demanding?).
- Build in a safety program and policies for alertness problems.
- Maintain cost neutrality.
- Develop a guaranteed vacancy coverage system (a method for covering sickness, vacations, jury duty, etc.) prior to implementation.
- Develop cross training.
- Adjust sick leave, vacation, holiday, and other leave policies.
- Revise break, lunch, and shift change policies to match a 12-hour work day.
- Develop a specific training schedule.
- Ensure communication and continuity of operation.
- Make sure exposure limits for noise, chemicals, etc., are appropriate for the new schedule.

One Manager's Perspective

Karl Meyers, the mill team leader (plant manager) at Ft. Howard Corporation (paper mill) in Muskogee, Oklahoma, has experience with many different schedule systems from both the shift worker and manager perspective. His plant recently changed schedules. Here are his thoughts on a variety of scheduling issues we have been discussing:

> I have worked for Ft. Howard for 22 years. The first 7 or 8 years of that was on shift work, both straight shifts and rotating shifts around the clock. It was the worst thing I've ever done in my life. I can remember the first time I was put on fixed 11 at night 'til 7 in the morning. I worked that for about 2 years straight, and it almost killed me. That's a strong statement, but it was very trying, and I never, ever felt good because I worked all week and then on Saturday and Sunday would try to go back

to being normal. It never worked. I always said to myself that if I ever got in a position to change it, I would.

When I came to Muskogee in 1978, we started this mill swinging so everybody would rotate through all three shifts. I felt that you had to give people something different because if you put them on straight shifts, the people on days were very happy, the people on afternoons were less happy, and the people on nights were always disenchanted.

Rotating shift work also is an advantage for the business. With fixed shifts, turnover rate and other problems are overwhelming. You almost have to rotate; otherwise you can't fill the night shift positions. You keep turning those people over. You spend a lot of money training, and there's a loss of productivity because of new people. It's always a problem.

We recently went through a major schedule change (168-44, balanced, 4-crew, 12-hour, rotating, combo), and at the same time we also started a quality process. Productivity improved. I'd say we easily got a 2 or 3 percent increase, even in the paper machines, our most continuous area. Absenteeism improved substantially—about 30 percent better. Turnover also improved, by 50 percent. That was a cost savings because we didn't have to retrain new people with the loss of good qualified people.

In the new schedule there are only two shift changes a day instead of three. Eliminating a shift change leads to a productivity improvement. This doesn't happen so much in the paper machine, because they run all the time, but it shows in the converting operation, where we make tissue, towels, and napkins. At a shift change you're not supposed to shut them down, but it's easy to do, so people would shut them down and talk. When we took one whole shift out, we picked up a productivity gain.

Not only that, but with one less shift we got better communication. This was a big one for us. Now we're dealing with only two groups of people, one-third fewer people, and we [management] could see both shifts every day. For instance, when I come in at 7:00 in the morning I see the night shift going home and the day shift coming in. We don't have that middle shift (the afternoon shift on the old schedule) of 8-hour people that I didn't see for a week or more.

The new schedule is easier to manage. We have constant everyday contact with our employees, and we handle stuff as it happens instead of letting problems develop—for example, machine problems, personnel issues, or just the ability to talk face to face. If they don't see you, shift workers forget what they want to tell you; when managers and shift workers can see each other every day, we pick up information that we would have lost.

We also built training into our schedule. We started it out with two very small areas with a total of about forty people. It works well. For the quality process I mentioned earlier, we wanted our work groups to meet a minimum of 4 hours per month to solve work problems and help make the business run better. We couldn't do it without these training shifts. These two areas started to make a lot of progress in resolving problems, and they are totally self-directed, without shift supervision. A lot of other groups have seen their progress and have asked us for a training day as well. Now, 90 percent of this mill—twelve hundred people—have a training shift.

The other major improvement is that people feel better. I've seen a whole attitude change. Mentally and physically they are more rested, and the shift workers are happier. They see their family life improved, and they are now back in the mainstream of society, instead of being out on the edge of it. Without changing the schedule, I don't believe we could have made the big cultural change our plant needed. This was a catalyst to kick off our whole quality process. It was a successful change that everybody in this mill was involved in and made the whole quality process and teamwork that followed it positive.

If you can't have people who have a good positive

attitude, how can you change the culture in your organization? You can't. I don't think we would have ever made
the productivity and quality improvements we made
without this change. It couldn't have been possible.

Weekend Warrior Model

An increasingly common method for 7-day coverage is the "weekend warrior" model: three crews work a 120-40 with 8-hour shifts,
and two new crews are hired to cover the weekends, working a 12-
hour shift on Saturday and a 12-hour shift on Sunday. For these 24
hours a week, the weekend crews may get 40 pay hours or be offered an opportunity to work more hours during the week to get
up to 40 work hours. Few continuous operations (those that must
run 168 hours every week) use the weekend warrior. Companies
that do use this model are usually businesses that started out with
a 120-40 and then saw a need to go to 7 days.

The weekend warrior model usually does not meet the three
key schedule design concepts. From the business viewpoint, it requires a staffing ratio of 5:1 (see Chapter 2), but the fourth and fifth
crew are rarely used effectively. Often these employees get a full
benefit package but provide only 24 hours of coverage. Typically
extra hours of work opportunities are provided to fill in the 40
hours as opposed to designing a schedule based on workload need.
As a result, idle time is frequently high, making this a costly option.

Another major problem is that the weekend warriors will not
be integrated with the rest of your employees. Being isolated from
management and the bulk of shift workers who mainly work
weekdays, they form a separate group identity and are not part of
the overall plant team. Their skill levels will likely be lower, and
communication, continuity, and productivity may suffer on Friday,
Saturday, Sunday, and Monday.

The term *weekend warrior* implies turnover. I've never yet met
a shift worker whose long-term goal was to work every weekend
and never have a weekend off. This may be a short-term goal, but
ultimately the weekend warrior is either going to quit or try to get
off the weekend shift, and management will continuously spend

money recruiting and training for weekend shifts. Still, in some situations this model may be the best solution—for example, if the positions require little training; if there is a part-time worker population, such as college students or temporary workers, available; and if the long-term needs are not a 168-hour-per-week schedule.

Because schedules are often copied from sister plants or competitors with little analysis, some of these problematic models are already becoming widespread. In the semiconductor business, a relatively new shift work industry, the weekend warrior model is already a standard. It is also more common in companies that have a strong human resources commitment to meet each employee's need. An organization faced with expanding operations may find it easier to provide coverage with part-timers and overtime volunteers rather than force current employees to work weekends. This is costly. In a department with 140 employees at one semiconductor plant, over $1 million was lost annually because of reduced productivity on weekends and the impact of the lower skills of the weekend warriors, which were felt on Monday of the next week. Implementation of an alternate 7-day schedule resulted in a 23 percent reduction in cycle time. Still, this schedule is being implemented worldwide although a few greenfield sites (new locations just opening up) are taking a closer look.

A semiconductor company in Ireland contacted us to design and implement a shift schedule for a new wafer fabrication plant. The existing plant utilized the weekend warrior. Our analysis showed that production on weekend shifts was only 43 percent of that during the week. Management had accepted this discrepancy because they could not force the weekend workers to come in during the week to train, despite the fact that they were dramatically less skilled. Management was pleasantly surprised when a rotating shift schedule that met all business needs was designed and was attractive enough to attract more than enough volunteers to staff the new plant.

Fly-In/Fly-Out Operations

With the increasing global search for new resources (minerals, oil, etc.), improved technology and communication, and time pressure to do it now, shift work is being exported to some of the most remote regions of the world. Shift work now is a fact of life in the North Sea, Alaska, Siberia, Northern Canada, the deserts of Saudi Arabia and Australia, and remote highlands of New Guinea, where native populations are being exposed to Western capitalism for the first time.

Companies at all of these remote sites want to maximize the return on their huge capital investment, but getting employees to work in these difficult environments can be a problem. Turnover often exceeds 33 percent a year, or a complete turnover in 3 years. These companies must find the best around-the-clock schedule. They must also consider transportation logistics (transporting employees in by bus, boat, light aircraft, or helicopter) and housing logistics (including building barracks, camps, or housing) as well. Hence, what is called fly in/fly out, or bus in/bus out, where workers are brought in for long stretches and then transported out for long breaks, is a new reality.

What is the best schedule for such an operation: 14 days on, 7 days off; 14 on, 14 off; 18 on, 12 off? The answer needs to be considered from all three design circles. For example, an oil company with multiple offshore platforms in Australia could save $15 million by staggering days off separately for each platform, thus significantly reducing its helicopter fleet.

Alex Heady is a shift worker I met returning from a consultation with a client in Papua New Guinea, one of the most remote and difficult fly in/fly out environments. (One company's mine on an island in New Guinea was taken over by local natives who shut it down and have seceded from the country.) I woke Heady up on the helicopter and plane ride back to Australia to find out why companies and shift workers work a fly in/fly out roster. Here is his answer:

> It's the only way you can work in the locale you are in. Nobody wants to live there. Anybody who takes the wife up there has got to have rocks in his head. It's as simple as that. It's unfriendly. It's not a safe place. That's why you've got to have a fly in/fly out. You cannot do without it. You could not live up there constantly. You've got to come back to civilization to get a quick breath of fresh

air, to bring you back to what reality is all about, before you can go back in again.

A while ago the police shot this bloke and then ran into the mining camp for protection. Hundreds of fully armed locals came in after the police. Our security lads were inside and when they tried to open the doors, there was just a mass of spears and arrows and everything flying at them, so they couldn't get out. The place was completely trashed. I was working underground at the time and that was a plus, because we've always said, if there is ever an attack, head for the mine, 'cause no one's too happy about coming underground. You've never seen darkness until you've seen total darkness, where you can actually put your hand in front of your face and touch your nose and still not see your hands; it's total blackness, there is no coordination, there's nothing.

I work in a fly in/fly out because, basically, I want a lot of money. I've got to admit to that, but the schedule is the big thing. You don't have a great family life when you are working this schedule. You're out of the country 8 months of the year. You've got 4 months a year off, but a lot of your time is spent traveling as well, so you haven't actually got 4 months of the year back home. You've lost a fair bit that way.

I work a 21/10, 21/9, 21/9, 21/12. [This means 21 days on—all 12-hour shifts—followed by 10 days home and so forth. The 21 shifts include a rotation from days to nights. Transportation home and back to work is provided for the 10 days off. The next sequence is 21 days on, 9 days off, and so on.] I have a break for a few hours in the middle when I change to night shift because I don't go in until the next night shift, but that's all. Twenty-one days is a long time. In the first week, it's fine: Everything is great, I'm back in, I'm fresh, and everything else. I've still got memories of being back home, and I'm happy with myself. By the second week, I'm starting to slow down. I don't get the full production out within the second week. By about the sixteenth or seventeenth day,

I'm getting very sluggish. By the last few days, anything will irritate me—literally anything.

This schedule is a killer. I'll get a call from supervisors saying, "Look, the machine won't start," and I get there and the operator is fast asleep! I literally have to shake him to wake him up—and this man is supposed to be driving an underground truck fully loaded.

I don't know who designed this schedule, but I don't think a great deal of thought went into it. It's always amazed me, because they've always said that the more remote the area, the less time you should spend there. Another mine was doing a 15-13. And yet our mine is a lot more remote, it's a lot more antisocial as far as lifestyle is concerned, and yet we go to a longer time on site. I just can't figure that one out. It's against all principles of the scheduling system.

A toned-down schedule would be great. If I stayed on the same money and went on a 15-13, you would have to pry me out of there with a crowbar because I would be as happy as a lark.

Fly in/fly out operations—shift work in remote areas where no one wants to live year round—will become more common in the next century. The more difficult the environment, the more difficulty in recruiting employees, the better the schedule must be. Schedules that maximize productivity on site and lower transportation costs, while maximizing time off and pay, can make these jobs more attractive. The cost of turnover and retraining can be enormous in FIFO operations.

Shift Schedule Circa 2000

Although no single schedule will fit every business, the following futuristic schedule includes concepts that can benefit you in the design of your ideal schedule. Remember that this model is not intended to be the answer for your business but rather a sample with various elements for you to consider. And remember that a model is not a schedule. This model can be worked with fixed shifts, only 2 consecutive night shifts, 7-day-a-week utility coverage, all 8-hour shifts, a 40-hour-per-week overtime policy, unbalanced coverage, 6-hour night shifts, and other variations.

Before getting started, let's summarize our major goals:

- *Business circle:* Low cost, reliable, self-regulating coverage that efficiently matches both core and discretionary workload.
- *Employee circle:* Excellent pay and time off so that shift work is more attractive than day work to maintain tenure and high morale.
- *Health and safety circle:* A schedule that allows circadian adjustment and minimizes sleep debt.

To maintain simplicity, let's assume our year 2000 business is open every hour of the year, requires balanced coverage staffing in the core operations, and the customer demand/workload is stable and nonseasonal. Furthermore, we want self-directed work teams cross-trained to handle production, maintenance, and administration of their own schedules.

In this model the workforce is divided into six lean crews. The normal staffing ratio of 4.2:1 (forty-two employees to cover ten around-the-clock positions) is supplemented with vacation and training relief operators, and there is elimination of overtime, supervisors, and separate maintenance workers. (A few maintenance specialists, instrumentation workers, and electricians would still be in the day maintenance department.) All employees are pooled and divided into six lean, skill-balanced teams. Therefore, the overall staffing level is equivalent to, or actually less than, a typical 168-hour-per-week operation. However, each crew is staffed so lean that if one employee is absent, the operation must shut down. Therefore, a high priority is placed on the shift workers to provide reliable, self-regulating coverage. This is the key concept in this model: Reliable cross-trained teams are rewarded with attractive time off.

Let's look down the schedule (Figure 5-5) for a snapshot view of 1 week for operations. On Monday Crew 4 is working 7:00 A.M.–7:00 P.M., and Crew 1 is covering 7:00 P.M. Monday until 7:00 A.M. Tuesday. Every day of the week two crews are scheduled to

Figure 5-5. An ideal futuristic schedule (168-40, balanced, 6-crew, 12 + 10 + 8-hour, rotating, "combo").

Crew/ Week	M	T	W	T	F	S	S
1	N	N	N	N	N	N	N
2	–	–	–	–	–	–	–
3	U_8	U_8	U_8	U_8	–	–	–
4	D	D	–	–	D	D	D
5	–	–	D	D	–	–	–
6	M_{10}*	M_{10}*	M_{10}*	M_{10}*	M_{10}*	–	–

$$D \ = \ 7 \ \text{A.M.–7 P.M. (first shift of week)}$$
$$N \ = \ 7 \ \text{P.M.–7 A.M.}$$
$$- \ = \ \text{day off}$$
$$U_8 \ = \ 8 \ \text{A.M.–4 P.M. utility crew}$$
$$M_{10} \ = \ 8 \ \text{A.M.–6 P.M. maintenance crew}$$
$$* \ = \ 20 \ \text{percent of crew has a day off here}$$

cover the core workload with 12-hour shifts, providing a total of 168 coverage hours per week. In addition, from Monday through Thursday a utility crew is scheduled in, and from Monday through Friday, a maintenance crew is scheduled in.

The utility crew provides 32 hours a week, which can be used to take vacation, cover vacation, cover sickness, train, engage in special projects, meet with customers and suppliers, or cover variations in the workload. All of these discretionary activities are now *scheduled* and are done at straight time. Notice that if an employee takes all 32 utility hours off, the result is a 14-day vacation (that is, the 7 scheduled days off, the 4 utility days, and the next 3 scheduled days off). A shift worker with 128 hours of vacation benefit (four 32-hour breaks) would be able to schedule 8 weeks of vacation. Of course, employees are not forced to take vacation in the utility week, and policies are set to provide coverage without overtime whenever vacations occur, by adding personnel.

The maintenance week is an opportunity for shift workers to work in maintenance or alongside a regular (day) maintenance crew. The goal is to develop a cross-trained maintenance-operation team crew, to pick up skills, and carry these skills onto the back shifts, hours where the technical-maintenance staff is not fully available. This built-in cross training should result in increased productivity, less downtime, and overall lower staffing for your business. Depending on the business, the M week could be used to work alongside sales, administration, engineering, or technical staff, depending on which skills you would like your shift workers to carry with them as they cycle around the clock.

There is no overtime in this schedule since it's a 168-40. Ideally, every employee would be on a salary package. Each employee is expected to provide 2,080 annual hours minus vacation. Assuming a pay rate of $10 per hour, the salary is $20,800; at $15 per hour, it would be $31,200; at $20 per hour, it would be $41,600; and so forth. Of course, the number of annual working hours can be adjusted up or down, and pay would change accordingly.

If your shift workers are on a salary package or are exempt, there would be no overtime. But even if they are hourly, nonexempt employees don't worry about overtime. This schedule requires the payroll department to pay out 240 hours every 6 weeks, equivalent to a normal 40-hour workweek. If you utilize pay factoring, you can follow all legal requirements without paying overtime.

Instead of adding shift differentials or weekend premium pay, we could add 80 hours of holiday benefit (the same benefit a day worker gets: pay for not working) to the vacation balance. Shift workers' holidays would be scheduled in the utility week. Remember, 32 hours of holiday time off equals another paid 14-day break, so this will easily be another 4 weeks off. If you are committed to a shift allowance or some kind of penalty to represent weekend and night work, why not apply these funds to a special health education program for shift workers (if the intention of the allowance is truly to deal with the problem of shift work)? This money could be used to facilitate good sleeping conditions such as airconditioning, sound baffles, light blockout, or housing assistance for situations where it's impossible for workers to find a quiet place to sleep or the commute is too long. In fact, this schedule would work best if sleeping quarters were located near the operation for the stretch of night shifts; employees could sleep there 6 days every 6 weeks.

From the employees' perspective the schedule is attractive. It provides 174 scheduled days off each year (most day workers receive 104), 35 weekends off each year (usually at least a 3-day or longer weekend), 8 or 9 full weeks off each year without using vacation, and vacation can extend four of these breaks to 2 weeks each. Flexibility of scheduling is enhanced by the degree of cross training and the ability to trade days off without management's permission. To maintain this type of schedule, shift workers are consistently responsible for coverage. Since there is limited overtime, the incentive changes. If an individual scheduled for a 12-hour shift is sick, someone from the utility crew must supply coverage by changing his or her schedule that week. Since "what goes around comes around" is the operating paradigm in this model (and there is no extra pay for the utility individual), the incentive is to cover each shift. Each team can work out its own utility crew rule, or there can be one overall policy for all crews.

From a health and safety viewpoint, the schedule has the unusual feature of working consecutive 12-hour nights. Can that be safe? Yes. Let's assume that our shift workers are exposed to bright light during the night shift to facilitate a rapid adjustment of circadian rhythm. Once the adjustment starts, it makes sense to keep the body rhythm adjusted to nights. During this 1-week stretch, which occurs only eight or nine times per year, the shift worker makes a commitment to be a night worker by sleeping 9 hours during the day, with minimal social life. (If this were an unbalanced schedule, which will become more common in the year 2000 with greater automation, shift workers might work only five or six night stretches per year, or split these nights into two 6-hour shifts.) Ideally, they would be driven from the plant after the night shift to a motel or barracks, where they would live for six days. The facility would have recreation facilities and dark, quiet, comfortable rooms designed for daytime sleeping. After the week of nights, there is a week off, and family-social life will assist a quick adjustment back to days. Furthermore, the shift worker does not have to deal with nights for another 5 weeks. (Again, this model can be changed to just 6-hour shifts and/or working only two or three consecutive nights.)

The remainder of the schedule is day shift—working either two or three consecutive 12-hour shifts, or four or five consecutive

8- or 10-hour shifts. Frequent days off will diminish the effect of potential sleep deprivation.

From the health and safety viewpoint, this schedule is like that of a U.S. tennis pro who must play one tournament every 6 weeks in Australia, comes back to the U.S. and takes 1 week off, and practices only 2 to 4 days in a row and rarely on weekends.

This schedule model has numerous variations. It can be a fixed shift system; it can be used for a Monday through Friday operation, for situations when a salary package is not legal, for unbalanced workloads, for situations when 12-hour shifts are too long or not desired. The model will still operate with the key principles of rewarding self-regulating schedule reliability with time off.

In Chapter 6 we will look at how to implement Best Cost Schedules. But before we get started, let's check in with Dick Scallan to understand how Renison got the right roster.

Getting the right roster for your crews is vitally important. You need to be sure you're doing the right thing. Even though your workers might suggest a roster, that might not be the best for your business.

The key point of our 10-hour shift underground was to have appropriate downtime to do maintenance and blasting, so when we operate, we are very productive. There was no point in going for the 12-hour shift because there would have been no gain. I'd still have waiting time with 12-hour shifts because I've got to have a shift change and I can't guarantee my blasting time exactly at that spot. I have to have the gear ready so that when they come on shift, they jump into a hot seat and are really revved up to get going. The workers knew we had to make a change—it was the only way we could stay in business. I had to increase tonnage, so I had to sell that to them. I told them the only way we could survive was to reduce our unit cost. If we didn't improve our productivity, we wouldn't be alive—we wouldn't have a future—we wouldn't have a chance.

In the plant we went to a continuous schedule with 12-hour shifts. It's a continuous, four-crew, 4 days on and 3 days off schedule. This reduced the number of times

we had to stop and start the plant and made us a lot
more effective. In engineering and automotive we put in
longer shifts to reduce set-up times, increase coverage,
and improve productivity.

Below are the solutions implemented at Renison:

Mining: 100-40, unbalanced, 4-crew, 10-hour, rotating, 4-3/
4-4/4-2.

Processing Plant: 168-44, balanced, 4-crew, 12-hour, rotating,
3-2/3-4.

Engineering: 52-42, unbalanced, 2-crew, 10- and 12-hour, fixed,
4-3.

Automotive: 120-40, balanced, 3-crew, 12-hour, rotating, 3-6/
3-2.

6

Implementing Best Cost Schedules

You will probably have only one chance to implement your Best Cost Schedule, so do it right. With this concept in mind, we flew to Tennessee to help an auto supply manufacturer that had just changed shift schedules. The employees were so upset with their schedule they were threatening to strike. Sometimes they even sabotaged the next shift's ability to produce. Managers were concerned because productivity had dropped and labor costs were up.

Arriving in Tennessee, I was surprised to find an excellent 168-hour-per-week schedule in place, one that is often considered a Best Cost Schedule by employees and managers in the auto industry. The problem was that management had made two implementation errors: the operations manager had unilaterally selected the schedule without any employee input, and one of the overtime pay rules had not been adjusted to fit the new schedule. So although the schedule was right, morale was plummeting, and labor was costing an extra $2.3 million a year.

The process of implementing a new schedule with the proper work, pay, and coverage policies is just as important as the schedule itself. Implementing new shift work schedules is like a game of chess. There are standard opening moves you can plan and principles to help in the middle of the game. Although the outcome is often unpredictable, appropriate preparation can lead to a favorable ending.

After watching many companies succeed and fail in schedule implementation, we have developed a change program with ten key components. The program is continuously being improved year to year and has many variations but as of now it looks something like this:

- Communicate properly.
- Analyze your business needs.
- Develop and cost schedule models that meet the business needs.
- Have employees assess the models.
- Educate shift workers and their families on health aspects of preferred models.
- Design the schedule(s).
- Develop implementation policies (work/pay/coverage).
- Build consensus with employees.
- Implement.
- Follow up.

This chapter will be divided into two parts. First, we will discuss change strategies. Second, we will come back to each of these ten components and explain them in detail.

Part I: Strategy

No matter what type of business you operate, understanding a few key implementation principles can guide you to a successful change. The first principle is "aim for success." This sounds like a simple concept but is the most frequently overlooked. Management must define its primary scheduling goals at the outset, so the entire organization is committed to making a change. Dean Rogers, a plant manager at 3M Company in Kentucky, told me that 70 percent of the top management team should agree to initiate any project, but then 100 percent support is required all the way to implementation. This is a good operating principle that we frequently recommend.

There are many roadblocks in the change process. A unified management team committed to success will overcome these obstacles every time. Without a strong sense of purpose, an entire project can be stopped at almost any time, by anyone, for any reason.

Some managers have no scheduling goals. Their credo is, "We don't care what schedule goes in as long as it doesn't cost more money." Whenever you hear that, expect implementation problems and a poor result. You would never say, "I don't care where my plant is located, as long as it doesn't cost more money," or "I don't care what piece of equipment I buy, as long as it doesn't cost more money," and "I don't care whom I hire, as long as it doesn't cost more money." All of these variables, including your work schedule, are essential building blocks of your business, which will have cost consequences in the future. A good schedule can save you millions; a bad schedule will cost you money.

Goals are different in different companies. Do you want to defer $10 million of capital expenditure? Improve employee morale? Build in training? Reduce lost time injuries? Be as specific as possible in defining your success or goal. "Reduce cost per ton to $18 within 90 days" is better than "lower costs." "Decrease operation logbook errors 20 percent" is better than "improve communication." And limiting success to a few key goals is better than having a long laundry list of objectives. For most companies, success will mean implementing a schedule that improves at least one index in the business, employee, and health and safety circles. We call this the Best Cost Schedule. The lowest cost schedule is not always the right schedule, especially if it has a tremendously negative impact on morale, and production costs ultimately increase.

A systematic approach that looks at all three circles will produce better results than a quick fix to a current problem, which may lock you into bad practices for the long term. Unfortunately, most facilities accept their current schedule system as a normal, unchangeable part of their business. Even if the current schedule is a high-cost schedule with low capital utilization, poor morale, and poor health and safety, it may be followed decade after decade unless a specific scheduling problem develops. As a result, many companies that consider changing schedules are responding to a crisis as opposed to a systematic, data-driven, engineered approach to finding the Best Cost Schedule for their facility.

Define Success Carefully

Should aiming for success solve the short-term crisis or provide the long-term solution? Here's an example of where management went with the short-term solution. A coal mine in South America was threatened with a costly strike because of a change in shift schedules. The mine is located in a remote area and most of the 4,000 shift work miners (Wayu Indians) live in villages 2 to 3 hours' travel time away. The miners were accustomed to being bused to the mine, living there in camps for 4 days, working 12-hour day or night shifts, and then being bused back home with 4 days off. In order to lower operating costs, the corporate managers in the United States instructed the mine manager to eliminate the camps, which meant employees would have to commute to and from their villages every day.

The day the camps were closed, management changed from the 12-hour schedule to a new 8-hour schedule. (An 8-hour shift surrounded by a daily 2- to 3-hour commute appeared safer than a 12-hour shift schedule surrounded by these long bus rides.) Days off were reduced from 182 per year to 91 upon implementation of the new 8-hour schedule. Immediately the employees went on a work stoppage, not because they were losing their camps but because they were losing their days off.

No production means losing big money fast and potentially losing customers. Management had to get these employees back to work. In just a few weeks we were able to work with the 4,000 employees, and resolved contract issues within their union. Two solutions were developed: (1) a 12-hour shift system without camps that would be safe for long-distance commuting and would get the shift workers back to work immediately, restoring normal production levels, and (2) a plan to maintain a mini-camp, create new work and pay policies, and potentially result in a 10 percent increase in productivity. Since success was defined by management as eliminating camp costs, the first plan was chosen even though it was not the best.

Changing your definition of success in the middle of a change program can be problematic. At one manufacturer in Virginia, the initial goal was to implement a more productive schedule that would improve employee acceptance of shift work and have less frequent rotation. A few months into the project, it turned out that a new centralized payroll computer system was the dominant variable. The goal of the project became to ensure that all schedules at the facility were changed to have a consistent start of the pay week on Sunday. All the alternative schedules that employees had supported had to be redesigned.

At a large refinery, management communicated to its union leadership and employees that the company was losing over $20 million a year due to operating errors (unnecessary downtime, equipment damage, etc.). A majority of the errors could be attributed to the lack of training for refinery shift workers, so the corporation decided to build regular training time into the shift work schedules. Employees and union leaders participated in choosing alternative schedules with built-in training time at the lowest cost and without disruption to employee time off. One day management received an industry report showing its refinery was overstaffed in comparison to pacesetting refineries. The entire shift training/rescheduling program was stopped indefinitely to focus on reducing manning levels. The shift workers and union are now confused about how important training and operation errors really are.

Spread a Wide Net

If you preselect a small pilot group of employees to make a schedule change, you can run into insurmountable problems. You may select a group that is negative to change or a group of converts lobbying for a particular schedule solution that meets only their potential needs, and then be forced to implement this schedule across the site. Other employees who want to change may feel left out. Rivalries between work groups may intensify, and so will rumors. The schedule in one department may not fit another. At Ralston Purina in Georgia, the warehouse was chosen as a pilot group, but since warehouse needs were much different from those of production, their popular new schedule was not made available to production employees. A better choice is to involve all employees from the start. Data collected from each work group will then help you determine whether to implement with only a small group, the entire plant, or a staggered implementation plan.

At Co-Steel Raritan, a mini steel mill in New Jersey, a new human resources management team was hired to improve employee morale and increase the level of trust in management.

Changing the shift schedule became one of their first priorities because time off on the old schedule was very poor. Of course, as soon as the new managers suggested a change, all of a sudden the shift workers seemed to like the current schedule for the first time. We met with over 400 shift workers at least five times each over 3 to 4 months, developing schedule options. Although the primary project goal was to make the shift workers happier, our data revealed that only one department, with just twelve shift workers, had enough trust to try a new schedule (one that increased days off without affecting pay or benefits). At this point I met with the president of the company, shook his hand, and said, "You have a major success here." You can imagine what he said to me when I told him that after all this time and effort, only twelve of his employees were changing. But our data made us confident we had selected the correct pilot group, and we had maintained our communication with the remaining 388 shift workers, telling them, "You don't have to change, but you still need to listen and understand the options."

Within a month, another 70 employees went on the new schedule, and within 4 months nearly all 400 employees were on the schedule. The transition was easy because all of them were involved in early communications. Morale improved dramatically. Even the most vocal, negative employee begrudgingly admitted to me, "The only good thing the company ever did was to put in the new shift schedule."

The Greater the Change, the Greater the Gain

The best schedule for your business is likely to be very different from your current schedule. Innovative schedules that require major changes are the most likely to give the biggest benefits. On the other hand, the closer the new schedule is to the current schedule, the easier it is for workers to accept. Implementing a current modified schedule (just a few features of the current scheduling system are adjusted) is easier but has a limited impact. In some companies even a relatively simple change—new shift start times, changing the direction of rotation, or a new vacation selection method—can create considerable controversy while not solving fundamental scheduling problems. Changing schedules is an emotional event for your employees, so you might as well tackle all of your scheduling problems at the same time.

Ask whether you want to make a small change or a big change. As a rule of thumb, aim for the greatest change possible, because you are not going to get all the way there anyway. Most organizations have a built-in inertia that limits change. On a scale from 0 to 100, with 0 being the current schedule and 100 being the perfect schedule, aim for 100, with the hope that your business will fall within the 80 to 90 range.

One Chance in a Decade for a Successful Implementation

A key reason to aim for a big change is that you may have only one chance in a decade for a successful implementation. If your facility attempts to change schedules and you are unsuccessful (you do not change at all or the new schedule is worse), everyone involved is likely to throw up their hands and say, "We tried scheduling, and it didn't work. Let's get on to something else." And since a schedule change can be such a hot employee issue (remember, you'll be affecting pay, time off, and family and social life), most managers do not want to tinker with it very often. Shift scheduling tends to be a slowly smoldering back-burner problem that comes to a boil every once in a while. Rather than wait for the pot to boil over, scheduling should be one of the continuous improvement objectives of a facility.

Don't Expect One Solution to Fit All Situations

A vice president of manufacturing read one of my articles on shift work and decided that all his plants should be on a 7-day schedule. He then picked a 168-42, 4-crew, 8-hour, weekly rotation, an old schedule we are most frequently asked by companies to change. (In his haste he had misread my article. I was using it to illustrate an outdated, poorly designed schedule.) Subsequent visits to several plants revealed that only one department in one plant had a need for a balanced 168-hour-a-week schedule. Furthermore, the employees in that department chose a 12-hour fixed shift option, not an 8-hour rotating option.

In 1994, I had the opportunity to work with Richard Trumpka, president of the United Mine Workers, along with the CEOs of four leading coal companies. For the first time in 50 years, language was placed in the nationwide union contract allowing each mine working with local unions and local managers to implement the schedule best suited for their particular business and employee needs. The agreement even allowed 7-day scheduling for the first time. In exchange, management guaranteed adding union members for locals going onto alternate schedule. Since the agreement, depending on sales, customer contacts, costs per ton, and equipment, we have recommended that some mines stick with what they have, some increase overtime, some go to 6-day operations, some to 7-days, and so on. Despite the initial impulse to jam in one 7-day solution everywhere, even mines within the same corporation typically need different schedules.

Communication

Another prerequisite to successful implementation is a strong education and communication program. Everyone involved in the change process needs to be continually educated and updated. Basic questions need to be answered up front:

- Why is the company changing schedules?
- Is the current schedule still an option?
- Who will select the schedule?
- What happens to overtime, premium pay, and benefits?
- Do all employees have to be on the same schedule?

Ideally, the organization (management, union, shift committee, consultants) chaperoning the change should communicate with the entire workforce, including those unaffected (e.g., day workers) by the prospective change. Communication meetings should be scheduled in groups, meeting around the clock in a short time period (24–48 hours) to stay ahead of the rumors. In our change program, we call the initial employee communication "rumor busters." If you understand the current schedule, the most common rumors can be anticipated. (For example, if your current schedule pays time and a half on Saturday and double time on Sunday, a likely rumor is management is just trying to eliminate premium weekend pay.) Therefore, it's best to answer the rumors before they even surface. For example, tell the employees whether the scheduling program is likely to increase, decrease, or maintain current levels of overtime. After your initial communication meetings, establish a hot line where any lingering questions, complaints, rumors, or criticisms can be responded to immediately.

Predicting what will happen next is another helpful technique. For example, inevitably at least one shift worker will pass out a schedule detailing how much money each employee will lose, even if it's a schedule option not being considered by management. If potential rumors are dealt with early on and consistently, their impact will be minimized. Within a few weeks, if your communication is direct and honest, employees will be listening to you, not to the rumors.

In our experience, there is no such thing as too much communication with shift workers. Frequently shift workers are accustomed to receiving their information from the grapevine instead of from management, who work primarily on day shift. The isolation created by most shift work schedules creates an optimal environment for "expert vocal critics" to flourish. These vocal critics can have a strong negative influence.

"Vocal critic" is a polite term. Many managers, shift workers, and even consultants use a whole host of terms to describe these individuals who are just dead set against change, no matter what you are trying to achieve. You may find yourself telling a group of employees, "We're considering trying a new schedule that will increase your weekends off and give you a 10 percent pay raise. You do not have to try it. If you vote to try it out and don't like it, at any time, even after the first week, you can go back to your current schedule." Normally, 5 to 10 percent of the workforce will immediately think you are out to get them. Often these employees may have a hidden reason to avoid changing schedules, such as a second job, a recent or upcoming shift bid, or maintaining extreme overtime, or they may just be against everything.

Not everyone who raises questions is a vocal critic. An employee who says, "I don't like this schedule because it interferes

with my family social life" or "The shift is too long" or "It interferes with child care" is voicing valid concerns that should be
brought to the forefront so that they can be analyzed and discussed. You can analyze different schedules and determine how
each affects babysitting, carpools, or college classes, helping employees to make the right decision for their needs.

Still, you will have to deal with these vocal critics. If you do
not have a plan to deal with the naysayers who are against you
every step of the way, your change program can be easily defeated.
The best method for minimizing their impact is to meet with shift
workers in group meetings throughout the change program, gathering data from each person but later feeding the information back
as group data. For example, when I am being harassed by the vocal
critics, I usually show a data chart from their department and say,
"Yup, this chart shows that 5 to 10 percent of you are against everything going on in this schedule program, but 90 percent at least
want to listen." Then I turn to the entire group and ask them what
they want to do: keep talking to the one outspoken individual or
move ahead and at least have me explain several schedule options?
In this manner, the group will force the vocal critic to fall in line.

Other techniques can be appropriate at times, such as allowing
these individuals to sound off. Other times they need to be confronted. Retelling classic stories exemplifying vocal critics is helpful, like the shift worker in Alabama who interrupted me to say,
"Don't even bother to show any rotating shift schedules around
here" and then 20 minutes later asked me to go back to that (rotating) schedule with 20 weeks off per year. I said, "Sorry, I can't
reshow that one because it has rotating shifts."

I've always been curious to find out what makes the most negative employees tick, and I found out one day at Barrick Goldstrike
Mine. We completed a very successful project at this Nevada mine
with over 90 percent employee support for the new 12.5-hour
schedule. However, throughout every meeting up to implementation, two male shift workers in their thirties needled and heckled
us every step of the way. Six months later, we went back to the
mine to do a follow-up assessment. Even in the follow-up meetings, these two hecklers continued being disruptive. Finally, at the
end of the last meeting, all employees were asked to turn in their
questionnaire, which ended with the question, "What do you like

better: the old schedule or the new one that you've been on for 6 months?" I glanced at their responses, and to my surprise, both had checked off that they liked the new schedule better! I threw up my hands and asked, "Why did you guys harass us for the last 12 months?" Their answer was, "Hey, we're known as the butt-heads around here, and we have a reputation to uphold."

It's often helpful for the managers or consultant to model both appropriate and inappropriate behavior. For example, if you find yourself becoming frustrated or make an unfortunate quip, you can quickly say, "You know, I was acting like a butthead right there." The audience will usually laugh and understand which be-haviors are considered appropriate and which are not.

Maintain Cost Neutrality

A key implementation principle for facilitating a smooth change is to maintain cost neutrality, defined as receiving the same pay and benefits for the same total work hours (Figure 6-1). For example an individual who works 8-hour shifts, Monday through Friday at $1 an hour, would make $40 for the week. On a new schedule working four 10-hour shifts, Monday through Thursday, cost neutrality sug-gests the employee should still receive $40 at the end of the week (even if your facility is required to pay overtime after 8 hours). If the employee ended up making $44 for four 10-hour shifts, this would not be cost neutral; the company would be paying more dollars for the same 40 hours of labor. The elegance of the cost neutral principle is that it is simple and understandable and avoids horse trading, which can be a tedious, confrontational process. There are a variety of methods, including pay factoring, whereby cost neutrality can be maintained without violating state law, fed-eral law, or union contract. (Pay factoring is when an employee's normal pay rate is adjusted down slightly so that the same pay is received for working the same number of hours over the complete schedule cycle.) There are also instances where overall it's best not to maintain strict cost neutrality—for example, when confronted with a difficult but overall productive shift schedule implementa-tion.

The cost neutrality principle becomes more complex when

Figure 6-1. Cost neutrality.

		M	T	W	T	F	S	S	Work Hours	Pay Hours
Current Schedule:		8	8	8	8	8	–	–	40	40
Various Options:	1a	**10**	**10**	**10**	**10**	–	–	–	**40**	**40**
	1b	10	10	10	10	–	–	–	40	44
	2a	–	–	**8**	**8**	**8**	**8**	**8**	**40**	**40**
	2b	–	–	8	8	8	8	8	40	52
	3a	**12**	**12**	**12**	**4**	–	–	–	**40**	**40**
	3b	12	12	12	4	–	–	–	40	46

In each of these examples, an employee works 40 hours per week. Depending upon whether overtime is paid after 8 hours, or whether Saturday and Sunday are premium days, the three schedule change options may be cost-neutral (requiring 40 pay hours) or may cost more for the same labor. (Cost-neutral options are shown in bold.)

dealing with more complex changes. Suppose a union employee currently works 20 percent overtime in addition to his or her 40-hour workweek. If the company goes to a new schedule that keeps the 40-hour workweek but reduces overtime to 5 percent, is that cost neutral? The employee will say "no," but the employer will say "yes." The employer is correct, if overtime is not guaranteed in the contract, but this must be properly communicated to the employee. Defining and answering these issues is critical for a successful and smooth implementation.

Suppose you are working 8-hour shifts, Monday through Friday, making $40 a week, and rarely working weekends. However, for the occasional weekend worked, Saturday is paid at time and a half, and Sunday, as the seventh work day, is paid at double time. You make $68 a week if you work both weekend days. Suppose the facility moves to a 7-day-a-week schedule, but your personal, new schedule is Wednesday through Sunday, with Mondays and Tuesday off. In the new scenario, you are still working 40 hours a week, so one could argue cost neutrality means your pay is $40, or one could argue that cost neutral pay should be $68 because Saturday and Sunday are overtime days.

Be careful how you define cost neutrality. At one nuclear power plant, the union changed schedules in 1988. The change from 8-hour to 12-hour shifts was not cost neutral, and shift work operators' pay increased 10 percent for working the same number of hours per year. Two years later the nonunion security department elected to change schedules. Department managers defined cost neutrality as receiving the same pay package as the union received. Corporate management was stuck with this decision since they did not want to take away pay or benefits from their security employees.

Consulting Versus Negotiating Approach

Implementation can take place using a consulting or negotiating approach. In a nonunion facility, use the consulting approach; in a union facility also try to use the consulting approach. The consulting approach is a schedule change based on consensus building with buy-in from all levels of managers and shift workers. Everyone helps build the solution, especially the employees who must work the new schedule.

In the negotiating approach, a few key individuals select one schedule. It's not uncommon for two lawyers meeting in a large city, hundreds of miles away from the factory floor, to select a schedule system and pay rules that affect thousands of workers and their families for their entire career. Sometimes two adversarial parties show up in a meeting room, and one party is armed with a new schedule the other party hasn't seen. The negotiators, who typically have only the briefest knowledge of shift work and scheduling, view the schedule as one chip in the overall negotiation that may cover ten or more other key items. The odds of meeting the needs of your business, desires of your employees, and health and safety standards will be stacked against you in this situation.

The negotiating approach is the right one to use if that's the way you normally make changes at your facility. But even in this approach, try to include all your employees in the selection of the types of schedule options to be negotiated and make sure the options meet your business needs. In this way you will be negotiating a solution that fits your situation. Too often negotiations simply start with the "answer" first (a schedule copied from another company), it's negotiated into the contract, and then managers and shift workers are left to figure out how to make it work after implementation.

If your facility is unionized but you cannot get your union interested in participating at all in a schedule change, don't give up. You still can build a schedule from all three circles. Fill in the hourly shift workers' needs by working with your shift supervisors. Communicate your progress on building the new schedule to all employees and union leaders each step along the way. Ask for input. When you have your answer, the Best Cost Schedule with appropriate policies, you can start negotiating your contract to implement changes. Often there will be a Best Cost Schedule within the limits of your current contract. At the same time, having an attractive option outside the contract ready to go (e.g., a schedule that adds union members, increases pay and time off, but improves productivity) may help bring the parties to the negotiating table. On the other hand, with some very strong, centralized unions it is best to start with national union leadership. If you can build a relationship that encourages win-win solutions, then their support will help make working at the local level possible.

Four Basic Change Strategies

In addition to the two major approaches, consultative and negotiative, there are four basic shift change strategies, shown in Figure

6-2. Do not begin a schedule change program without defining which category you are in.

Type I: Do Not Have to Change/Cost Neutral

In a Type I program, pay and benefits are kept cost neutral, and the current schedule does not have to change. The employees may be involved in the process of evaluating and building schedule options and selecting new work and pay rules, but at any time before scheduled implementation, shift workers can say, "Never mind, I don't feel like changing." Without giving any explanation, they can elect to stick with the current schedule. Then the shift schedule change program is over. Furthermore, if employees elect to change in a Type I program, there is usually an option to go back to the old schedule after a trial period.

Because employees hold the veto switch, controlling the decision to change, Type I programs generate the highest degree of employee trust. In our experience, employees will elect to change schedules around 90 percent of the time in a Type I program, especially if the new models are more attractive (with more time off) than the current schedule. Although the employees have a great degree of control over their fate, this does not mean that the new schedules are being designed solely according to their preferences. The schedules still need to meet all three design circles.

Figure 6-2. Four basic shift-change strategies.

Current Schedule Status

		Do Not Have to Change	Have to Change
Pay and Benefits	Cost Neutral	I	II
	Take Away	III	IV

Not surprisingly, the primary goal of many Type I schedules is to improve employee morale, but management also has a tremendous opportunity to build its business needs improvement into the schedule design. Ft. Howard Corporation in Muskogee, Oklahoma, carried out a Type I project that maintained all shift work penalties such as Sunday premium pay. The employees did not have to change but all 1,000 employees elected to change schedules to improve time off (the employee circle). However, since the new schedule was partially designed on the business need to reduce both shift changes and the start-up and shutdown of equipment and to increase communication, productivity also went up about 2 or 3 percent.

Type II: Have to Change/Cost Neutral

When CCG began shift work consulting in 1980, the majority of clients wanted Type I projects. Now, most of our projects are Type II projects. In a Type II project, the current schedule is no longer an option because it does not meet the business needs and/or is a high-cost schedule, so change will occur. From the employee viewpoint, Type II projects are typically greeted as both bad news (we must change schedules) and good news (but pay and benefits will be cost neutral, and we can help pick the new schedule). Sometimes these changes are "cost plus," with the new schedule resulting in a pay increase for shift workers while improved productivity decreases overall costs for management.

Success in a Type II project is largely determined by how unified the management team is on the need for change and how well management communicates its rationale for change to the shift workers. One Midwest food manufacturer was running a 168-42, 4-crew, fixed, 12-hour schedule with an "every other weekend off" (EOWO) day-off pattern, a popular schedule among their employees. But skill balance and quality were so poor on the night crews that management was convinced that they needed a rotating schedule. The core management team was unified on this principle because their cost analysis showed millions of dollars were being lost under their fixed shift system.

The plant manager met with all of the first-line supervisors to explain the findings and the reason for change. She then asked them to make a presentation to the top management team, showing how they would communicate this need for change to their shift work crews to support the change. This was not easy! Senior shift supervisors, who had finally made day shift after years of night shift work, were required to tell their entire day shift crew (all senior employees) that fixed shifts were not working and a rotating system was needed. Whenever the supervisors wavered, management reemphasized this was a Type II, must-change project. Because of the unity and communication, a very unpopular change from a schedule system that had been in place for nearly 65 years occurred in just 12 weeks, quickly and with excellent results.

In all shift change programs, not only do you need to educate and communicate the business needs for change, but you should measure the effectiveness of your communication by asking your employees questions that will indicate whether they understand the need for change. If approximately 80 percent of the workforce understands the reason for change (not agrees, but understands), then you can move ahead with schedule selection and implementation. If you have not obtained the employees' understanding of the business reasons for change, they will fight every new schedule solution.

Figure 6-3 shows employees' comments from a Type I and a Type II project. Employees were asked, "Why is management considering alternative schedules?" In the Type I project, employees got the answer right, indicating the primary reason was to improve morale, but the other two circles (health and safety and business needs—i.e., to improve productivity) were also correctly seen as major drivers. Only 2 percent of the employees said that it was to reduce overtime (the wrong answer), and a small percentage had no idea what was happening.

The shift workers in the Type II project in Figure 6-3 also were correct. Only a small percentage of employees stated the goal was to improve morale or health and safety. Most understood that the major goals were to increase productivity and to lower costs and improve competitiveness. These feedback results were sufficient to proceed with the review of schedule models with employees in both projects.

If your feedback results indicate poor understanding of the project, then you have problems. For example, in a Type II project,

Figure 6-3. Employees' responses to why management was seeking to change the schedule.

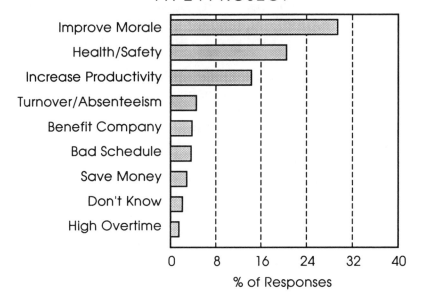

TYPE I PROJECT

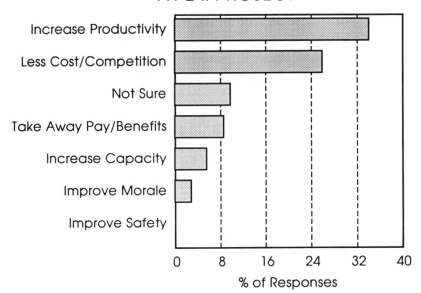

TYPE II PROJECT

shift workers may not understand the business reasons for change, or in a Type I project, employees may think it's a "take-away project." You should be concerned if over 20 percent of the workforce has no idea why the company is changing schedules. You then need to go back and communicate the basic reasons for change before evaluating schedule models. Do not be afraid to feed back to the workforce even the most negative comments. If some employees say the reason the company is changing schedules is "because the company is a bunch of dummies" or "to take away overtime and make our lives miserable" (recent comments we have recorded), post these comments on the bulletin board. Your credibility and chance for success will improve.

Remember that in Type II programs the current schedule is not discussed or offered as an option. Here are a few last tips. Let employees know who is driving a Type II program. Usually it's the customer demanding lower-cost products, better quality, more hours of availability, and faster delivery.

Type II programs often turn out to be a win-win situation for managers and employees. A common Type II program is for a facility to change from 120 operating hours a week (24 hours a day, 5 days a week) to 168 operating hours a week (24 hours a day, 7 days a week). At ATR Wire & Cable in Danville, Kentucky, each employee who underwent such a change received 78 additional days off and a 7.5 percent pay raise. Overall productivity improved, and overtime went down.

After a Type II program begins, employees typically see that their job is more secure by working a schedule that saves the company money and solves a critical problem. The fully utilized plant is normally the one with the best job security.

Type III: Do Not Have to Change/Take Away

In Type III programs, the schedule does not have to change, but there is a take-away of pay and benefits. For example, a facility may take away Sunday pay, reduce overtime, or restrict shift and job bidding because of the high cost and constant retraining of the workforce. In a Type III program, although you don't have to change schedules, it may be advantageous to improve the work schedule. Employees who are accustomed to bidding out of bad schedules by moving to other shifts or departments may be restricted from bidding for several years. At the same time, when you restrict bidding, consider changing the work schedule to make the time off and pay attractive enough to keep employees in their current positions.

Alumax Mill Products, an aluminum sheet rolling mill in Lancaster, Pennsylvania, was a Type III. A very competitive business, the mill reduced premium pay on weekends, which resulted in an average annual pay reduction of $5,000 per employee. Employee morale declined, and complaints about the rigor of their schedule increased. It became apparent that the schedule had always been a problem, but previously shift workers hadn't complained because they wanted to preserve the premium and not rock the boat. Once premium pay was eliminated, management hired us to determine if better schedules existed for the employees with the hope that their involvement and satisfaction would rebuild some of the lost morale. As expected, when the project started, there was tremendous resentment toward management by shift workers. However, after an employee involvement–schedule implementation program, all twelve departments elected to change schedules. Ten departments opted for the new schedule with a long break, and two went for a modification of their current schedule. The results were increased credibility for management and a change in attitude. The premium pay take-away is now generally viewed by employees as necessary to stay competitive. In fact, nearby companies have recently had layoffs, and one plant is in danger of closing.

Type IV: Have to Change/Take Away

Type IV programs—the schedule must change and pay and benefits are also reduced—can be the most painful program. In these programs, management must communicate the business reasons for change and point out the take-aways.

At an air-conditioning manufacturer in Ohio, employees were forced to go from a 5-day-a-week schedule to a 7-day-a-week schedule that eliminated premium pay on Saturday and Sunday. The employees and union had no choice in the matter. The communication was simple: "If you don't make this change, the plant will be closed down and the work moved to our Mexico location."

But even in such dire circumstances, the goal is still to implement the best possible 7-day schedule and seek employee involvement. Type IV projects are most appropriate when the issues are cost-cutting, survival of the business, loss of customers, or a reduction of the workforce.

It is difficult to finesse these tough changes, and many managers wish to make a bad situation for employees look like a good one. At one manufacturing plant where we were facing a hostile group because the goal of the program was to eliminate Sunday premium pay, a shift supervisor sincerely trying to help interjected, "CCG is only here to help you feel healthier on shift work." We had to disagree and tell the audience, "Actually, we're here to figure out the least painful way to take away overtime." Being honest and direct with a good reason for change will ultimately lead to a winning solution.

Premium Pay and Overtime Pay

A common management goal when changing schedules is reducing or eliminating premium pay (extra pay linked to specific days or hours) and overtime pay (extra pay for working more than 40 hours in a week).

There actually are a number of options for dealing with premium pay and overtime pay without damaging employee morale.

1. *Don't change it.* Keep the policies the way they are. In industries where labor costs are a small component of total costs, the benefits from the improved schedule may far outweigh any cost savings from changed pay policies. However, in other situations, maintaining your current policies may be cost prohibitive and make you uncompetitive.

2. *Take premium pay away.* In certain circumstances it's best to make a clean break from your current policy and eliminate premium pay. This decision will be based largely on the rationale for change. Mead Johnson's old plant in Michigan had a 5-day-a-week master operating schedule, with weekend work paid at time and a half for Saturday and double time for Sunday. When a new $120 million plant was opened next door to the old one, management

simply announced that this plant was designed to run continuously 7 days a week and there would no longer be premium pay for weekends, since the old policies were based on a 5-day-a-week operating strategy. Since the organization was also preserving existing jobs and adding more than 100 new ones, the employees accepted the change with hardly a comment.

3. *Implement a buyout plan.* Baker Refractories, a brick manufacturer in Pennsylvania, implemented a buyout plan to phase out Sunday pay. One small department of shift workers was already working Sundays and being paid double time; now the entire manufacturing department would be working Sundays, so management projected employee earnings for weekend work for the next two years and gave all employees extra salary. Effective that same day there was no more Sunday premium pay.

4. *Wean employees from overtime.* Implement a new schedule, but understaff each crew. Guarantee employees the opportunity to make their normal amount of overtime or premium pay by volunteering to come in on their days off to cover the holes in your schedule. The results are fairly predictable. In the first quarter, the opportunity to make the same level of pay will reduce anxiety caused by the policy change. The entire workforce will show up to get overtime pay on their days off. In the second quarter, only half the workforce will show up. By the third month only 10 to 20 percent, the true overtime hogs, will come in. Most of the workforce will prefer to wean themselves from excessive overtime to obtain time off, and management can gradually add staffing to the short crews.

5. *Modify your overtime policy.* If you are working Monday through Friday with Saturday at time and a half and Sunday at double time, you might consider paying time and a half after 40 hours and double time for hours 48 through 56. This is closer to cost neutrality, and your business can go from 5 to 7 days a week without being penalized for weekend work.

6. *Build overtime into the new schedule.* Your new shift schedule might have 41-, 41.6-, 42-, or 48-hour workweeks even though your premium pay policies, as such, have been eliminated. Built-in overtime guarantees shift workers extra pay in their pocket, and usually more money than they receive now.

7. Average the workweek over the shift cycle. This is done in many foreign countries, especially in heavily unionized industries, and allows for much more creative, flexible schedules, including the concept of salary packages for union employees. A salary package essentially pays a shift worker an annual salary for working an annualized number of hours and is likely to include some built-in overtime. If you develop a salary package, make sure you already have your Best Cost Schedule determined; otherwise your built-in overtime dollars may not be utilized at all.

Combinations of these approaches can be tried as well. In summary, a variety of methods is available to change your premium and overtime pay policies without making the consequences negative for your shift workers.

Shift Committee/Team/Task Force?

The first instinct of many companies considering a schedule change is to put together a shift committee, team, task force, or some other group made up of representatives from each shift work crew, or in a union operation, representatives of management and the union. Shift committees often start by collecting schedules from nearby plants, or they may evaluate a schedule generated by a department, a petition, a lone enthusiast, or someone new to the plant who worked a schedule elsewhere. They may also collect articles about shift work and attend seminars. Most of the schedule options that shift committees develop are employee driven and based primarily on the employee circle, so opportunities to meet the business needs and find cost savings may be missed as the momentum to hone in on "the schedule" takes precedence.

As a rule of thumb, shift committees don't provide the best solutions. Many of them seem to behave like the U.S. Congress: a collection of special-interest groups all looking out for themselves as opposed to the common good. The first day I walked into one power plant, which had eighty shift workers, I was greeted by a group of approximately twenty individuals—the shift committee. My immediate thought was that the odds of implementation would be very slim; there were too many people on the committee. Each person represented himself and perhaps a mate. One shift worker announced he was on the committee to make sure the plant didn't change schedules; another was looking for the best schedule to work a second job.

Shift committees often have trouble looking at all three circles with a balanced viewpoint. Often management sets the team up to focus primarily on the employee circle, since committees are usually given boundaries (e.g., no increase in head count or costs) instead of a list of improvement possibilities. That's a mistake; the Best Cost Schedule may include hiring more people or paying people more in order to increase productivity dramatically, reduce overtime, or defer capital expenditures.

There is one last reason for a nonunion plant to avoid a shift committee, which by definition will be discussing hours of work and pay: You may be violating National Labor Relations Board regulations, and your shift committee may have the official legal status of a union.

Shift committees can work well in union shops. If you implement a schedule change in a union environment, you will usually want to have involvement of the key union leadership at the site. Since hours of work and schedules are almost always part of the contract (even where management clearly has the right to change schedules at will, in practice the union may need to be included), it's possible some contract language will need to be amended if the new schedule falls outside the current contract. In that case, it is beneficial to assemble a shift committee of union and management leaders.

Their role, however, is not to *choose* the shift schedule. The union-management shift committee should act as a vanguard for change and review contract issues in case any policies or schedules are outside the current contract. They may need to draft a letter of understanding needed to implement the new schedule. For example, "Employees in Department X can try out the schedule for one year, with the following new policies, but both union and/or management can return to the current schedule if the following events occur." Then a series of criteria is defined.

In this fashion, we have had many shift committees successfully work as change agents. Most unions agree with this approach, letting the membership choose the schedule If the union leaders select the new schedule, they run the risk of not having the support of their membership. An ideal shift committee should have no more than six members: three union and three managers. On the union side should be the leading, ranking officials at the site who can make decisions. The management side should include one operations and one human resources representative and one first-line shift supervisor who has credibility with the union and shift workers.

If you are forming a shift committee, don't put together the same people who negotiate all of the contract changes, especially if they have had an adversarial relationship, and don't hold the meetings in the same room as the one where negotiations take place, because this environment will lead to the same type of negotiating stance. A good working shift committee looks at data together and plans how to achieve a smooth implementation. The actual solutions are data driven and based on the needs of the business and employees, not based on the personal preference of the committee member. It can be very difficult for shift committee members to switch out of the role of decision makers. A neutral third party is especially helpful when a shift committee is mandated and previous collaborations have been more negotiative than consultative.

At one U.S. refinery there was great animosity between management and labor on the six-person shift committee because a senior human resources manager saw his role as picking the schedule and protecting the company's position, while a union representative (who didn't even work at the refinery) saw his role as fighting the company. Every time the group met, the atmosphere was one of negotiation. The human resources manager was eventually replaced by another human resources representative who was not as tied into negotiations, and the meetings were moved to another room. With no one to fight, the outside union representative stopped attending the meetings, and eventually a spirit of cooperation developed. The committee felt it was their role to convince skeptics, in both the union work force and management ranks, that a change would be positive for all parties.

The committees that are most successful look at all three circles and develop a process of change that involves the entire workforce. Others spend three or four months researching information and gathering nearby schedules, but they are unsure how to proceed. The more time that goes on, the more pressure they feel from the floor, until a schedule is selected. Occasionally, we have seen shift committees throw up their hands, desperate for help. The shift committee at British Petroleum in Lima, Ohio, decided to disband itself. The head of the union said, "I think it's dumb for us to be messing around with schedules when there is obviously such a better technology for making changes." A shift committee that finds itself in this position should put a trusted manager, an internal consultant, or an outside neutral third party in charge of the shift change project so that the process can move forward.

Part II: Components of a Basic Change Program

Everyone wants a Best Cost Schedule—the one that meets the business needs at the lowest possible cost with high employee morale and excellent health and safety. Once you've decided changing schedules is a priority at your location, you need a game plan. No two organizations will get there in exactly the same way, but there is a process that typically leads to a successful implementation program.

Step 1: Communicate Properly

For starters, communicate properly. Tell your employees why your facility is considering a change or is changing schedules: whether it's a Type I, II, III, or IV program; whether a shift committee will be established and who will be on it; and the reasons for change. Discuss key rumors and rumor busting, your timeline for change, who the decision makers are, and so forth. Employees need to be told what their involvement will be in the change program and where management will be the key decision makers. If management already has the answer—usually a mistake—it's better to say so than hide it.

Step 2: Analyze Your Business Needs

As you analyze your business's scheduling needs, consider these questions:

- What is the core and discretionary workload?
- Can idle time and overtime be improved?
- Is the workload balanced or unbalanced? Does it fluctuate?
- How is the current schedule working? Is it completely broken, or can it be modified?
- Is keeping the current schedule an acceptable alternative for the stated business objectives?
- Where are the cost saving opportunities?

Step 3: Develop and Cost Schedule Models That Meet the Business Needs

Once your business analysis is completed, build several schedule models (remember from Chapter 5 that a model may have tens, hundreds, or even thousands of derived schedules). All of these models should be acceptable from the business viewpoint. Then figure their cost. Most companies will be comfortable developing approximately six models for a department, which encompass a wide range of options. Although the models are driven by an operational/statistical analysis, try to anticipate basic employee desires and build in parameters that provide health and safety. The business needs analysis is also an opportunity to look for scheduling problems or glitches that can be solved. Is there a more effective way to coordinate maintenance and operation schedules? Should supervisors always work the same hours as the hourly work force? Is there a better way to schedule breaks and lunches?

Step 4: Have Employees Express Their Individual Desires

After the management team has selected and costed alternative models, the models are released to the shift workers. Management has set the menu; now the employees who will ultimately work the schedules can review and evaluate them, indicating those that look most attractive. In addition, their personal schedule desires are investigated so that later on, the models can be turned into the schedule(s) that best fit(s) their needs. Our extensive shift worker database helps us pinpoint needs. Figure 6-4 shows the results of

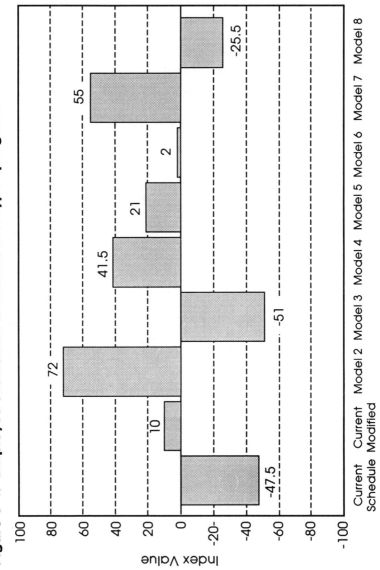

Figure 6-4. Employee evaluation of models in a Type I program.

an employee evaluation of the models in a Type I program (notice the current schedule was an option). Shift workers preferred models 2 and 7. In feedback meetings these shift workers were told that all their schedule options would be based on these two models, with the actual schedules designed based on modifying the models to meet the individual preferences that were also tracked. It's complicated: Each model is rated on a 4-part scale, and each scale is given a weighted value. The higher the score, the greater the chance of successful implementation.

When determining model preferences, track not only whether employees like or dislike the schedule but also include how strongly they like or dislike it. These evaluations should be compiled by department or natural work groups because frequently different models will be implemented in different work areas. Remember that it is appropriate to have different schedules if department workloads are different. If the workloads are the same, it makes more sense to have the same schedule for ease of administration.

When you meet with your shift workers, don't just show them the models, provide them with a complete explanation. For example, let's say the goal of model 2 in Figure 6-4 is to increase equipment time on paper machine 12. Explain how the model works, then present comments from other shift workers who have worked this model and liked it as well as those who disliked it. Then be prepared for a host of questions. For example, an employee may want to know, "Could the Sunday shifts starting at 3:00 P.M. be 12-hour shifts starting at 7:00 P.M.?"

Often employees ask more complicated questions—for example: "What happens if on Sunday night, at 11:00 P.M., I'm supposed to be on funeral leave, but at the last minute, I'm called in to work 4 hours to cover a vacancy? What is my overtime meal pay allowance that night on model 5?" The appropriate answer is, "I have no idea right now. Just let me know whether you like the model enough for us to work with those details later." Do not try to select a schedule the first time you show a series of models. Find out which models employees like, determine their concerns, and later on build a schedule from that model to fit their needs. And remember that all the models that shift workers are evaluating have already been approved by management.

In a Type II, III, or IV program, you are likely to have many employees focusing on their current schedule and rating all of the new models low; they're still dreaming of keeping the current schedule. In that case, the appropriate response is, "That's no problem. If you don't want to rate any of these models, or you want to rate them all negatively, management will pick the schedule for you." Employees usually realize then that they need to rate the models. After they have done so, the results are analyzed and fed back to the employees. Remember to collect some open-ended comments from the employees and continue to measure how well you are communicating the reasons for change.

Step 5: Educate Shift Workers and Their Families on Health and Safety

Once your employees have rated the models, it is a good time to bring their families in for education sessions, emphasizing the health and safety circle and putting all three circles together. We have found that trying to provide education for adjusting to shift work without changing schedules is often futile; few will listen, and even fewer will change their habits. The employees have been on their current schedule for a number of years, and they are already expert at coping. When employees are considering a change to new schedules, you have a small window of opportunity—a time when they will listen to an outside third party or an expert about how to cope with shift work. After they are on the new schedule for 6 months, it's probably too late.

Step 6: Design the Schedule(s)

Now specific schedules are drawn up. For example, if employees like model 2 but stated preferences for longer breaks, earlier starting times, and oscillating shifts, the model is adjusted accordingly. Once the models have been adjusted, you will typically have a few leading schedules that have the best chance of implementation success.

Step 7: Develop Implementation Policies

Now is the time to anticipate the work, pay, and coverage policies that will need to be changed to fit the new schedule. For example, if you are changing from Monday through Friday 8-hour shifts (for a total of 40 hours), to Monday through Thursday 10-hour shifts (still a total of 40 hours), how do you handle pay in the ninth and tenth hours? What rate do you pay for working Fridays or Saturdays or Sundays? What happens if a vacation day is taken on Monday: Is it charged at 8 hours or 10 hours? How will a last-minute sickness be covered on the night shift? Will the new schedule require more cross training or job rotation? All of these issues need to be worked out before asking employees to make a final schedule selection. A mistake here can torpedo all your previous efforts. (At one East Coast power station a change in schedules was not successful because early on during the trial period an error by the accounting department resulted in incorrect paychecks.)

Step 8: Build Consensus With Employees

Putting this information into a document or implementation manual is the next step. An implementation manual is a document that shows the new schedule(s) with every work, pay, benefit, and coverage policy clearly spelled out, together with comparison tables to the current schedule. These are no longer models but finalized schedules. Never ask a shift worker to make a final decision or to vote on a schedule until the implementation manual is completed. All policies and answers to questions such as funeral leave are detailed here, and employees will know exactly what they will be voting for.

Don't just hand out the implementation manuals. That's an invitation for more rumors. Meet with all the shift workers in group meetings, and go through all of the major points. Then pass out the manuals and have a question-and-answer period. Most employees are ready to fill out a ballot at that meeting.

Many companies are sensitive about the term *voting*. But as long as the employees are selecting schedules based on the models approved by management, why not let them select the schedule?

In a refinery in South Africa in 1991, every shift worker was allowed to vote on the new schedule. One 40-year-old shift worker was extremely thankful and told me this was the only time he had voted in his entire life.

Americans are used to voting on everything, and U.S. shift workers readily accept this concept. On a typical ballot for a Type I project, the employees will be asked if they want to change or keep the current schedule. They are then asked to select their favorite alternative. Even an employee who elects to stay with the current schedule has the opportunity to vote on a favorite alternative, in case the majority of the workforce opts to change. In Type II and IV programs, employees are asked their number one choice from several alternatives, but the current schedule is not included. Normally there are no more than two or three schedule options on the ballot. We call these schedules, not models, because now the specific pattern for a whole year, with all the policies and potential impacts, is spelled out.

Another frequent point of debate is what percentage of employees are required to change schedules. Companies have invoked all types of odd rules. One management team in Alabama who really did not want to change schedules required an 80 percent criteria for change. (They didn't change.) The steel workers' union at one location allowed us to meet with their members only if 100 percent of the shift workers in a department voted to change schedules, before their schedule program even began! (They did change.) Some managers have argued that there needs to be a two-thirds or 75 percent vote. The most valid and widely supported principle is to require more than 50 percent of the workforce to agree on a schedule. If you allow employees to help build the schedule, the percentage is usually much greater than 50 percent. During follow-up, 6 to 12 months after the new schedule has been worked, we usually find 70 to 90 percent preferring the new schedule over the old one. (Remember that in a presidential election, a 55 percent–45 percent vote is considered a landslide!)

A couple of techniques are important to building a strong plurality.

- Schedule implementation meetings at the plant at times convenient to each crew. (If possible don't hold the night shift over.)

- Have makeup sessions for employees unable to attend, and designate a hot line or a key person (manager and/or union leader) for employees to contact with questions.
- Do the actual balloting at the implementation meeting where all of the information is presented. Have someone present who can answer all questions about the implementation manual so employees are making an informed vote.
- In a union operation, review your balloting procedures to make sure they are not self-defeating. (In some situations, the union's voting mechanism is set up so a group of maintenance day workers who regularly attend meetings at the union hall will vote down a schedule change for shift workers who can't attend day meetings. And the change has no effect on the maintenance day workers!)

Step 9: Implement

Once the balloting is completed, select an implementation date. Often the employees are asked what date is good for their needs. A schedule can be implemented on any date, but there may be optimal times from a business viewpoint, or what we call "natural implementation dates": January 1, after summer shutdown, after a holiday period, at the beginning of a pay period or before the busy season. As soon as employees have made a decision to change schedules, the goal should be to make that change as soon as possible so the vocal critics don't step in. If employees need time to establish new child care, classes, or carpool arrangements, a 60-day waiting period is usually appropriate.

When you are changing schedules from old to new, you may need to develop a special transition schedule. At Tenneco in Louisiana, for business reasons, the schedule needed to be changed around November, which would have a big impact on the shift workers' holidays. One crew that was finally getting Thanksgiving and Christmas off after missing them for 7 years would miss these holidays again on the new schedule, so a special transition schedule was put in place to preserve the holidays for this crew. There are also transitions where there may be a slight increase or decrease in pay for one or two crews. At Conoco, in Billings, Montana, once the union leadership realized that one crew could lose 8 hours of pay in the transition, they reasoned, "Oh, that's the reason why management has been trying to change schedules." In fact, there was an easy solution to this issue, and it was offered to these employees: "Anyone who is short on work hours will be offered the opportunity to come in at their convenience to make up these hours."

Despite all your planning, once you start working the new schedule, minor glitches may surface such as: how to cover, perhaps, or pay for an unusual vacancy or workload change. Normally there is some type of ongoing mechanism, such as the management team or an outside third party, to solve these problems as they arise. Surprisingly, the actual schedule changes usually proceed smoothly. Any "trauma" has already occurred.

Step 10: Follow Up

It does not make sense to ask employees early on how they feel about their new schedules because they are still reacting to the change, not the schedule. Wait 6 to 12 months. If you ask employees in a Type II or IV program about their schedule, make sure you don't listen to any comparisons to the old one because it's no longer an option. In the most difficult of change programs, it may be best to avoid any follow-up at all. Instead ask workers, "Considering the options you had, what do you think of the new schedule?" And it's better not to ask any questions at all than to ask the wrong question. At one manufacturing plant that had been a Monday through Friday shift operation for years but recently went to continuous shift work, employees are given an annual survey that includes the question, "What don't you like about your job?" Every year since they went to the continuous schedule, the answer came back, "Shift work." Now they have a documented "shift work problem."

In a Type I program, do a follow-up survey, ideally after 6 months to a year or after employees have gone through a complete cycle. Find out how they like working the schedule once they have gone through all the seasons of the year, from a family viewpoint, and taking the school calendar into account. Also, follow up on your business and health and safety statistics. If the overall results are good, stick with your new schedule. If they are only fair, further modify the schedule. A similar follow-up may or may not be appropriate in Type II, III, or IV projects, because there's no option to go back to the current schedule.

When will you see the results of a schedule change? Most of the benefits of the new schedule occur quickly. If the new schedule forces you to utilize your best equipment more hours, or if it reduces idle time or increases production hours, expect improvements right away. If your schedule design was based on improving morale, then the changes may not become evident for 3 to 6 months or until the employees have had enough time to change their family and social lifestyle to match their new schedule. A common misconception is that productivity improvements occur because the shift workers are happier with the new schedule. Happier employees may or may not produce cost savings, and it's possible they won't be sustained. That's why the best schedule changes are structural ones that encompass all three circles. If you design a schedule that reduces costs or increases efficiency and the employees are also happier, and it's healthy and safe, you've done it. You have a Best Cost Schedule. As soon as you implement, your cost savings will start accruing.

The subjective benefits to the health and safety circle normally appear right away. If employees were used to working 7 or 12 consecutive shifts with rapid rotations and are now working two consecutive shifts with fewer rotations, they will report they feel much better on the new schedule in the first month. Objective improvements in health and safety statistics may take a longer time to surface. If lost-time accidents are measured in thousands of man-hours, it may take a year or two to spot a trend. Absenteeism typically goes down after implementation but may go back up a year later depending on the policy you have in place (if you allow 5 paid sick days and use overtime to cover sickness, you will probably average 5 days of sickness per shift worker). Employees' evaluation of the schedule will often change with time. In the first month or two on the new schedule, the employees are not so much commenting on the new schedule as they are on the difficulties they are having changing their outside lives to match the current schedule. Remember that most of these workers have become experts over time at the old schedule, mapping out their family lives, social lives, child care, school, sports teams, and television shows, and now they are being asked to make a complete change.

Almost everywhere I go, the minute I start talking about implementation, someone in the audience will explain that the reason implementation is difficult is that shift workers resist change. My experience shows this is not true. Shift workers don't resist change, they resist *being* changed. Involve them in the process, show good schedules, and you'll find them willing to change.

Clyde Williams is a president of Union Local 1-5 of the Oil, Chemical and Atomic Workers Union in Martinez, California. His duties include negotiating contracts and policies. He has been involved in shift committees that made schedule changes. I asked him to review his implementation experience.

The old schedule at our refinery had been around a long time. It was a nightmare. We had 8-hour shifts with backward rotation, and on Sunday we had to work 16 hours with only an 8-hour break and then get back to work. It was really a hectic schedule. People hated it.

Eventually some of our members filed petitions for 12-hour shifts, so the bargaining committee went to the company to try to get some conversation started on them. Management didn't want to talk about it, but we said, "Let's go and see what's out there." I was neutral when we started looking into 12-hour shifts. I knew it was difficult to commute on an 8-hour shift system and that there are fewer commutes on 12-hour shifts, but Dave Cauldell, who was on the committee at the time, saw you on television and gave you a call. We were allowed to get help, so we called Coleman Consulting Group.

Our shift committee was made up of three management and three union representatives, with Coleman Consulting Group facilitating the process. The refinery's upper management thought it wasn't going to work and couldn't be done, but the shift committee came together and convinced top management and other union representatives who thought it wouldn't work.

The union had some difficult pressures! Some union

leaders took the international union stand that we could not work anything over 8 hours. They said the members really don't know what's good for them, and we should just stick with 8 hours and call it quits. As the bargaining agent for the members, we could have gone along with this, but naturally the members would have been upset.

Everybody needs to be involved in this kind of change because there is a part of the 12-hour scheduling that meets employees' needs, but you then have company needs and health needs. You have to look at all three of those and see if they meet your criteria.

Our implementation approach was a turning point. I guess that was the first thing union and management actually worked out and talked about outside the contract. We didn't do the schedule change at contract time; we did it while we had a contract. It opened up the avenues of communication, and the relationship with management has actually gotten better and better.

I think you need to keep your schedule change off the bargaining table because it's a complicated process. There are too many details that you have to get right. Trying to do it all during negotiations would be difficult and would cloud the whole bargaining process.

Before the new schedule, we had a lot of people requesting transfers out of shift work. But once they got into shift work, they were locked in. Management just wouldn't let you go, so a lot of people quit. Now we have people transferring from maintenance (day shift) into operations (shift work) to get the new schedule. If you come out here and talk about going back to the old schedule, they would kill you!

Now we're interested in getting some dedicated training time, which the shift committee is working on, and we're pretty close to wrapping that up. Scheduled training time is important because of a new safety law that the Occupational Safety and Health Administration came out with. A lot of training and employee involvement needs to get done to comply with that law.

There is no way you are going to make shift work

totally perfect. But we're talking about 95 percent of the folks here that enjoy their schedule.

The Situation at Renison

Finally, I asked Dick Scallan to summarize his experience and results at Renison.

There was such a deep-seated resistance here. The workforce had such bad experiences with management in the past that it was really bruised and battered. I wanted to do this schedule change as best I could, and I needed a good system and an ethical means to the end. I was able to consider options that I may not have considered and was advised as to what was the best thing to do and what was not quite the best thing to do.

I think the increase in productivity has been significant, but most important, the schedule helped us achieve our vision. There was only a very remote possibility that we could get a new shaft in the mine to make a future here at Renison. It was more likely that unless we established ourselves and improved our game, we would close down in 1995 or 1996. We had to change a lot of the ways we were mining, and in so doing we were able to save significant money.

With exactly the same number of employees, we've increased productivity by 17 percent, and we've been able to show the world that we've got the right attitude, and we're determined to succeed.

Based on this success, I am pleased to tell you that three weeks ago Renison's board approved a capital expenditure of $34 million, which will allow us to keep this mine operating into the year 2020 and possibly longer.

Index